Erasmus Henry Brodie

Euthanasia

A Poem in Four Cantos of Spenserian Metre

Erasmus Henry Brodie

Euthanasia
A Poem in Four Cantos of Spenserian Metre

ISBN/EAN: 9783744760638

Printed in Europe, USA, Canada, Australia, Japan

Cover: Foto ©Thomas Meinert / pixelio.de

More available books at **www.hansebooks.com**

EUTHANASIA:

A POEM IN FOUR CANTOS OF SPENSERIAN METRE

ON

THE DISCOVERY OF THE NORTH-WEST PASSAGE

BY SIR JOHN FRANKLIN, KNIGHT,

'the first that ever burst
Into that silent sea' (*Coleridge*).

BY

ERASMUS H. BRODIE

ONE OF HER MAJESTY'S INSPECTORS OF SCHOOLS.

LONDON:

LONGMANS, GREEN, AND CO.

1866.

PREFACE.

HERE are two, I scarcely know what to call them, notions or prejudices, which the writer of a poem of any length and pretensions in these days may expect to hear quoted. The first of these is that somewhat vague and general assertion that our age is not a poetic age, that rather it is a great epoch for practical efforts and results of every sort, a hard-working utilitarian time, devoted to manufacturing, engineering, trade, commerce, and political economy, but alien in its instincts and tendencies from poetry, with neither leisure to cultivate it nor inclination to attend to it. No very logical and precise answer can be here attempted to such a statement. 'Solvitur ambulando.' For my own part (let others answer the objection as they think best), so far as I claim to be a poet, and may therefore feel an interest in the truth of this matter, I will plead my belief that, even if all this be granted, still Poetry 'is not dead, but sleepeth;' that, so long as our human nature and instincts remain

the same, so long as the world continues to be, what, in
one form or another, it always has been, a great stage of
acting and suffering, of sublime endurance, lofty resolu-
tion, passionate endeavour and perpetual struggle, so
long will true poetry, which is the verbal incarnation of
these deeds and thoughts and scenes, command attention,
and awake a faithful echo in man's heart.   But the poetry
must be good in its quality, true and human, and not
merely beautiful, but, as Horace says, sweet also with a
certain winning charm and grace, such as lovely flowers
seem to have, independently of their beauty of form and
colour.

So I have wished, nay so I have striven, to write ; with
what success let others judge.

The second notion, alluded to above, is more specific
and precise, and cannot be so easily dismissed.   This
does not object to poetry, but to the poem, as regards
the subject chosen, and asserts that no poem of any
length, that is of the epic nature, can be really great or
interesting, unless the event of which it treats be distant
and remote, in time at least, if not also in place.

Since all the greatest epic poets, to say nothing of the
great dramatic poets of Greece, favour this belief by the
example of their practice, selecting for their subjects
events either much anterior to their own times or
altogether removed from the terrestrial sphere—while
Spenser, who really described the moving panorama of
his own age or of that immediately previous and passing
away, transported his scene to Fairy Land, and wrapped
his characters in allegory, thus obtaining the same effect
—no one can deny that the notion which I have referred

to must be based mainly on truth. Doubtless, to quote
the well-known line, in this case, as in many others,

'Distance lends enchantment to the view.'

The exalted imagination sees with very different eyes
the common occurrences of every-day life, so seemingly
dull and trivial, so seemingly insipid and tasteless
(though even from these our best novelists can paint
charming pictures and construct tales of exciting interest),
and those great events of historic import ' Portions and
parcels of the dreadful Past,' which have long found
their recognised place of honour in the vast drama of
the ages. Doubtless, looking up from the hum and buzz
of the world around him, and fixing his gaze on some
memorable exploit of the mighty dead—' The Crusades,'
' The Discovery of America,' ' The Death of Montezuma,'
or ' The Fall of Wallenstein'—the poet feels himself free
from shackles and fetters, nay even from certain technical
difficulties and obvious hindrances, which might hamper
and impede him in treating of the present, especially
when at once so well-informed and so minutely critical
as is ours to-day.

The boundless expanse of the infinite, the Alpine
elevation, the larger atmosphere and region of grandeur
and sublimity, to which the poet, bent to raise, enlarge,
inform, purify the souls of others, must constantly ascend
and re-ascend, can doubtless be more easily reached from
a starting-post selected on account of its very nearness
to those spheres, than from one surrounded by living
voices, and, as it were, in the heart of modern London.
Yet poems have been written, and far from unsuccessful

ones, on events either very recent, or even cotempora-
neous with the writer. Such a poem was the noble and
patriotic 'Persæ' of Æschylus; such again was Lucan's
'Pharsalia,' a work marred indeed by the luxuriant
extravagance of early youth, and wanting the severe
revision of experienced taste, but full of nerve, vigour,
and the fire of genius, moving us in its best passages to
high admiration if not to rapture. One of Byron's most
touching and effective descriptions in 'Childe Harold'
is the account of the scenes just before and after Waterloo
—an event then (when the poem was published) but of
yesterday, and on which Scott wrote a poem of some
length in his happiest style, with picturesque effect and
such patriotic ardour that it cannot be read without a
glow of pleasure by Englishmen. A poor array indeed
this to set against Homer, Virgil, Dante, Tasso, Spenser,
Milton, yet enough to prove that, though a poem of the
highest order, a national epic could not be written on
some very recent event, it is not impossible to write
a poem of real interest on such a topic. The poet,
then, who does not aim so high as to write a great epic
poem, but who yet seeks to interest his readers by the
narration of some great event, need not be debarred from
selecting that event from among the exploits of his own
times. If he be a true poet, his instinctive vision will
direct his judgement to divest his subject of all that is
trivial, to dress it in its true dignity without the exag-
geration of false colours, and communicate to it that
living existence which the vivifying imagination alone
bestows. Let him not be too disturbed because the
public are previously familiar with all the details of his

subject, and will criticise it the more minutely. Rather let him rejoice to have a cultivated audience, and spectators all the keener and more attentive because, to speak a little vulgarly, so well posted up in the facts. For whatever poetry is henceforth written, and however, it seems to me, that it must at least be produced with a more constant perception in the author's mind of the audience to whom it is addressed, and in a more self-conscious spirit of its purport and nature, I say not therefore with greater effort or less spontaneity (for the poet alone, and not the versifier, will still be the poet), nor with an offensive obtrusiveness, but still with that allusion so eloquent to the wise, those subtle associations which speak only to those that can hear. So much by way of protest against that prejudice which I have described; now let me add a few words on the poem itself, at once the cause and illustration of my remarks. The discovery of the north-west passage by Sir John Franklin (for his prior claim over the no less resolute and daring McClure has been clearly substantiated by McClintock's researches) may fairly be considered a great event, nationally great, historically great, nay even of world-wide importance. For after those wonderful scientific discoveries and mechanical inventions of our epoch, which have produced and are still constantly producing results so stupendous and so fruitful, nothing in the long run has done more to link together the nations of the world, and to establish on a securer foundation those bonds of peace and commerce which are now hopefully bringing different races to understand and appreciate one another, than those pioneers by land

and sea, who have undergone for this cause countless toils, and endured every kind of privation, illness, and suffering. Livingstone, Grant, Speke, Burke, Wills,* and our long list of maritime discoverers from the Cabots, Baffins, Frobishers, down to the Parrys, Rosses, Franklins of our own day,—what a tale of heroic adventure, of unequalled achievement ! The north-west passage indeed can never be of any practical utility, and it will doubtless seem to many that all the toil and trouble has been endured in vain, and noble lives idly lost in a fruitless enterprise.   In no such light can I regard it, nor in such a light, I am satisfied, do our splendid English seamen regard it.   For in the first place it is something to have settled the question, and to have obtained for England the honour, though a barren one, of having done so ; secondly, it is no little result to have made such immense additions, as the voyages in the Arctic regions since the year 1818 have made, to almost every field of knowledge, geographical, ethnographical, zoological, meteorological, and others.   In these voyages and in that of Sir James Ross to the Antarctic both magnetic poles have been discovered, and many most important phenonema relating to tides, currents, winds, configuration of land and sea, formation of ice, and kindred topics noted and ascertained. Surely it is desirable that, as mere inhabitants of the globe, we should study to know all we can about its wonders and secrets in every part.   But to me there seems a yet greater importance attaching to these and

* Having lately read his most charming, most interesting book, let me add the name of Palgrave.

similar voyages and expeditions. They are the school
of our national spirit, and, in a somewhat luxurious and
utilitarian age, keep alive that old love of adventure, and
contempt for danger and no less for ease and comforts,
which possibly indeed, pushed too far, may run riot
in romantic extravagance, but which it would be an ill
day for England to see extinguished. Besides the
national, and, I may add, the cosmopolitan importance
of my subject, one other advantage accrues to it. It is,
so far as I know, a fresh field. The maritime glories of
England, whether of war or of discovery, have not been
celebrated as they certainly deserved to have been.
Beyond Campbell's famous and spirited Ode, and Falconer's 'Shipwreck,' I know of nothing written on the
subject, and the latter is in no sense national, and not
interesting. As regards the story which I undertake to
narrate, whether I have succeeded in narrating it well
or ill, others will judge. If I have not, I alone am to
blame, not the story. For it is richly fraught with the
materials of poetic interest. The national longing to set
the question at rest, the enthusiasm on the departure of
the Erebus and Terror with their gallant crews, the
confidence reposed in the captains, the devotion of the
men, their prosperous voyage, the last glimpses of them
in Baffin's Bay, their lengthened absence, the uneasy
surmises and first trembling anxiety about their fate, the
imagination transported to that lonely Arctic scene, the
wild exciting long-continued chase, resulting in nothing
but the discovery of their first winter quarters, the fearful tale sent across the Atlantic by Rae, the abandonment
thereupon of the search by Government, and finally the

heroic efforts and devoted constancy of Lady Franklin, crowned by the successful yet melancholy discoveries of McClintock, all these successive events constitute a drama of unequalled and almost breathless interest. Franklin himself, who discovered that which it was the aim of his life to discover, and then died still hopeful, before inexorable fate had overtaken his men and involved them in so fearful a catastrophe, we may certainly pronounce happy. But not even his men would I pronounce unhappy, in spite of their fearful sufferings and melancholy death. Doubtless to them—

> ' One crowded hour of glorious life
> Was worth an age without a name.'

But into this matter, from a consideration of which the title of my poem ' Euthanasia' is derived, I need not enter further here, having written some preliminary stanzas on the subject.

The poem will finally consist of four cantos. Only the first is now offered to the public. The second is now finished, but still needs some pruning before publication ; the third is more than half written ; of the fourth, parts are done. The hope of the author is to publish the whole by Christmas 1866. Though the ' nonum servetur in annum ' of Horace has not been observed, it is now six years or close upon it since accident first directed the author's attention to the subject of the poem. But the ' secessus et otia,' which Ovid rightly claims as the needful conditions for the gestation of poetry, have been wholly wanting. Official work and other interruptions have distracted attention and impeded all continuous progress. Still the poem, though repeatedly laid aside as regards its actual execution, has been scarcely a day out of my thoughts during these years, and perhaps its quiet basking in the still light of imagination has been of more service to it than a quicker progress.

The stanza of Spenser on which the author at last alighted, and then wondered why he had not first chosen it, seems well adapted for a narrative poem. Its versatility suits the most animated movement or the most pathetic pauses, and melancholy cadences equally well. Moreover, while each separate stanza presents a complete idea or miniature picture, all so lend themselves to the general effect, and promote the progress of the whole, as wave after wave imperceptibly hastens the in-coming tide. But though I use the stanza of Spenser, I have not therefore, as others, using also his stanza, have done, affected his archaic words, phrases, and inflections. My poem relates to what is wholly modern : modern too should be its dress. Rather have I humbly sought to learn the melodies, to catch the spirit, to imbibe the wisdom of the mighty master, than to array myself in his exact garb, and to dress in his very fashion. So much by way of a ' tedious-brief' preface. Would it were shorter, but how hard is brevity !

My thanks are due to many, both persons and books— first to Lady Franklin, to whom, when the whole poem is published, I am kindly permitted to dedicate it ; next to her niece, Miss Cracroft, and to Captain S. Osborn— for much information most kindly given ; to the works of Sir L. McClintock, Simmonds, R. Brown, the deceased Scoresby, F. Mayne, and many others. The admirable pictures of Mr. Church, the American, have also aided me much in realising the scenery of the Arctic regions, especially as regards icebergs and the Aurora Borealis.

E. H. B.

Manchester :
Nov. 1865.

EUTHANASIA.

———◦——

CANTO THE FIRST,

DESCRIBING

THE DEPARTURE OF THE CREWS OF THE 'EREBUS' AND 'TERROR.'

'One equal temper of heroic hearts.'—TENNYSON.

———•◦•———

I

Go now, my ship, launched on the public sea,
That silently hast grown in secret dock ;
Nor axe, nor saw, nor hammer fashioned thee,
Hewn by poetic hand from lifeless block ;—
Go and expect the rude affronting shock
Of waves and winds, and elemental jar,
Nor shame thy parent soil and British stock,
True heart of oak, hight ' Euthanasia,'[1]
Following the bear with sev'n lamps and steadfast star.

II

Hight ' Euthanasia,' the death of bliss,—
For while I cast about to find thy name,
This, that, the other, all did sound amiss,
Nor any fitly marked thy proper aim,—
At last into my pond'ring mind there came
That old-world tale of the Athenian sage,[2]
Who one of seven shared high wisdom's fame,
And to king Crœsus, richest of that age,
Spake wondrously, so tells the grey historic page.

[1] Euthanasia means a happy death.　　[2] See Herodotus, Clio, 29–33.

B 2

III

For when he asked, who was the happiest,
Showing him all his treasures, all his gold,
With secret wish to be pronounced most blest,
Then answer made that other, wisely bold,
Nor heeding aught his pedigree unrolled,
But far postponing purple Lydia's pride,
Of Tellus first the aged Athenian told,
Falling victorious on his country's side,
Next of the God-loved pair in painless sleep who died.[1]

IV

Full wisely well he spake, and as a friend,
Who, disregarding past and present rate,
The rather looked how fared it to the end :
So searching archives hoar of ev'ry state
Might I the changeful chance and final fate
Of many mourn, whose bright ascending sun
In cloud of darkest dole set soon or late,
Yet others too might find, whose life begun
Toilsome and hard perchance, constant and true did run.

---

[1] Cleobis and Biton, who having performed a signal act of piety towards the goddess Here, afterwards expired without pain, as it were in a blissful trance, in her temple. I am well aware of the grave historical doubts thrown on this recorded interview of Solon with Crœsus ; but these do not in the least affect the moral, nor my application of it.

V

Meseems such crown of bliss gilds that brave crew
Of waveworn mariners who sleep afar;
'Twas theirs, what many longed t' have done, to do,
Then death o'ertook them; now exempt they are
From toil and trouble, life's unceasing war,
Unenvied in success, a happy band,
By Franklin guided to the polar star,
Their courage by his ardour fed and fanned,
Performing vet'ran old what erst his boyhood planned.

VI

The golden sunshine dropping thro' the trees
Is sweet, sweet the birds' voices in the glade,
Or that deep murmur of alighting bees,
Sweeter where thick o'er-arching boughs have made
A chequered interchange of light and shade,
To cite swift thoughts from memory redeemed,
Or muse high poesy with fancy's aid;
But sweetest 'tis to be what once we seemed,
And live in manhood's hour as childhood brightly dreamed.

VII

Such lot was Franklin's; him the bounding wave
From life to death entranced as with a spell,
It was his world, and now it is his grave,
For whom winds, waters rang the fittest knell.
Thou weatherbeaten tar, God rest thee well!
'Tis thine to sleep in bliss, thy toils are done;
'Tis mine to patriot ears thy tale to tell;
Ah! task too hard, by me too bold begun,
Still must thy fame so fast this feeble quill outrun.

CONTENTS OF CANTO I.

EUTHANASIA.

CANTO I.

I

EXPLOITS marine, heroic deeds, I sing,
An arctic tale of England's grief and pride,
Borne far, beyond supreme imagining,
To songless wastes, of poet yet untried,
Forlorn, and bleak, and nipp'd by wintry tide;—
So strong a pity melts my troubled soul
For those brave tars, our countrymen, who died
Where stiffened lands and frozen billows roll,
Rough wilderness of ice around the northern pole.

II

Let others war inspire, and war's proud spoils;
Me gentler thoughts engage: my virgin rhyme
I dedicate to those who bore all toils,
Winds, waves, sharp famine's pang, the joyless clime,
That they might crown the latest aim of time,
And knit Atlantic to Pacific wave
By the long sought-for path; with hope sublime
For this they faced the pole, for this they gave
Freely sweet life away, and made the snows their grave.

III

Too long o'er Europe's war-tormented plain
Red Carnage had outpoured his lava flood,
Blackened the wasted fields, and piled the slain,
A bloody banquet for his cormorant brood;
Too long for peace to one the world had sued,
But sued in vain; then swift uprose at last
Celestial Vengeance in her justest mood,
To his lone isle caged the fierce tyrant fast,
Discrowned and baffled there to ruminate the past.[1]

IV

As when sharp Winter with congealing breath,
Usurping Spring's dominion, checks the year,
Locks up the torpid lands in icy death,
And chafes th' inactive farmer filled with fear
Lest barren snows should never disappear;
Sudden the south lets loose a genial breeze,
At once the skies, at once the meads are clear,
Carol the blithe birds from the greening trees,
Rich gardens burst in bloom and hear the hum of bees:

[1] During the long war, however much scientific inquiry may have progressed by means of learned societies or private research, it could not necessarily obtain much aid from the government, straining all its efforts to crush Napoleon. But on the return of peace every branch of science was stimulated by public as well as private effort, and maritime discovery, the favourite field of British enterprise, was vigorously prosecuted, chiefly through the exertions of the late Sir John Barrow. The first Arctic expeditions, however, did not take place till the year 1818.

V

So, almost in despair, Hope's self had fled,
Nor dared men say that rest would be restored,
The rolling drum such constant panic spread,
So long had pealed the cannon, flashed the sword,
And deadly havoc's fiery tempest roared :
But lo ! fair Peace returns, and with her leads
Ethereal Wisdom by best minds adored,
Who quickly sowed in ready soils the seeds
Of loftiest desires and exemplary deeds.

VI

She, high inspirer of the human breast,
To fame and labour spurred the noblest hearts,
And still into her eager service pressed
Each finest soul endowed with choicest parts ;
With some to subterranean pits she darts,
Secrets of ancient mystery to probe ;
Others on ardent voyage swift she starts
To every nook of this wave-girdled globe:
These weigh transparent air, those sift light's fairy robe.

VII

To heaven's far flaming floor her spirit flies,
Searching the clouds and azure as she goes ;
Thro' earth she pierces with a million eyes,
And views all marvels that her caves enclose,
And day by day some fresh discov'ry shows ;
Sans horse o'er land, sans sail speeds over sea,
Or mounts the skiey mountain's lonely snows,
Measures the rolling wave's velocity,
Or scans thro' darkest depths all forms of life that be.

VIII

She first o'er trackless wastes and torrid sands
Ardent explorers sent with purpose keen
To learn the varied tale of distant lands,
And what the history of each had been,
To note what beasts, what plants might there be seen,
That kindly trade might join the sundered shores,
Nor waters roll a barren waste between,
That hiving knowledge might increase her stores,
And sager grow the mind o'er life's vast whole that pores.

IX

Chiefly our sailors went at her behest
O'er ev'ry sea ; for, on adventure set,
Still Britons love the tossing billows best,
And those the most where danger most is met.
Hence, navigated last, least known as yet,
The polar ocean, white with ice and snow,
Wondrous, attractive, wooed them, a new debt
Owing to enterprise : all longed to go
And see the skin-clad men, seal-hunting Esquimaux.

X

To whom unknown the race of Esquimaux ?
'Innuit' they call themselves, whose frozen land
Denies subsistence ; they enduring go
West, north, and east, an always-roaming band,
Where'er thro' icy walls the waves expand,
In 'baidar' light or vaster 'oomiack,'
And hunt for seals along the frosted strand ;
Almost the seal supplies their ev'ry lack,
Or, where lakes near the coast, the scented oxen track.

XI

Their manners strange, how ev'ry gift they lick,
Needle, or saw, or looking-glass, or knife;
The conjurors, who tend their old and sick,
Striving by song to stay the ebbing life,
And hunger bear, and lash apart in strife
Their frames, and thro' them bullets fire unseen;
Their arts, their arms, old rites with wonders rife,
I pass, inclined, did time admit, their clean
Pure dome of snow to sing, and winter's household scene.

XII

Their chiefs direct them and distribute food,
Whom lesser chiefs, sage elders, still attend;
By their commands the voyage is renewed,
Or the fresh march at proper times they wend.
Their far progenitors, they say, ascend
Back to the moon; but Providence and God
Are words unknown; whence sprang, and what shall
      end
Mankind, they not inquire, but careless plod
Life's dull dark round, then sleep for aye beneath the clod.

XIII

But not to see the Esquimaux alone,
Nor icebergs, nor the flushed Auroral skies,
Nor all the marvels of the arctic zone,
Tho' fraught with perils, rich with novelties,
Charmed thitherward our seamen's eager eyes;
What most allured them was discov'ry's fame,
For England and themselves to win the prize,—
This kindled in their hearts adventure's flame,
Imperious honour's hope, ambition without blame.

XIV

Long had the wisest mariners believed
That by north-west a passage might be found
To Asia's shores, and shorter this conceived
Than that which leads by Afric's southern bound
To Indian seas, a long and dreary round;
And now that calm was to the land restored,
Again of voices keen was heard the sound,
Urging that cape and bay should be explored,
While vacant hours allowed, nor war's harsh tempest
    roared.

XV

Promptly the nation gave its willing ear
To such appeals, and backed with gen'rous aid
A cause to science and to glory dear;
Fresh expeditions constantly were made
Year after year, and winters whole men stayed
In frorest deserts, roaming with the gun
After what deer or arctic foxes strayed
Coursing the solitudes, untaught to shun
Their human foes, nor saw long months the absent sun.

XVI

'Twere tedious to narrate what all endured,
Or fitly proper praise of each decide,
Else Parry long to winds and waves inured,
Parry five times by polar horrors tried,
Or Rosses twain, by blood and deeds allied,
I'd sing, Back's, Beechey's, Lyon's feats sublime,
A hundred more, whose fame spreads far and wide;
Enongh,—them only I embalm in rhyme
Who, cold and far off, sleep in hyperborean clime.

XVII

Since Parry first westwards from Baffin's bay
Victor o'er ice and snow securely sped,
And on thro' Barrow's straits pursued his way,
Full many a tar, by his example led,
Here, there, had sailed, and named gulf, isle, and head;
Others, descending rivers, gained the coast;
So knowledge of the seas and shores was spread,
But still what science longed to know the most
Lay hid, nor any could the proud discov'ry boast.

XVIII

But what was surmise once was now belief;
' The passage must be found,' such rose the cry,
' Hazard one final last attempt;' the chief
Spokesman was Barrow, whose sagacious eye
Pierced the whole matter, prompt his memory
Recalling every voyage spurred his breast,
With wit by failure sharpened still to try,
Himself in ardent youth disdaining rest
Had sailed Spitzbergen seas, and tow'rds the pole had
  pressed.

XIX

Nor less was he deep versed in nature's laws,
Of currents much, and much of ice he knew,
Wise for high purpose, not for vain applause,
His stores of learning were excelled by few ;—
Now round him sit captains of many a crew,
Inconstant ocean's old familiar friends,
And science too surrounds with vot'ries true:
To him about to speak th' assembly bends,
And nods th' assenting head, and rapt attention lends.

XX

He thus, his soul by both ambitions fired,[1]
The thirst of knowledge and his country's praise,
Spoke, and achievements maritime inspired :
' Once more, my countrymen, my voice I raise,
' Raised oft for the same cause in bygone days ;
' Little, it seems to me, nay nought is done,
' If that, which sums the past, still mocks our gaze,
' And we must still deplore each setting sun
'That nearer brings the goal, but leaves it yet unwon.

XXI

' What in the morn of manhood we pursued,
' A glorious aim, in life's autumnal day,
' With stronger reasons, firmer faith endued,
' Shall we forego, and with experience grey
' Let others bear from us the palm away ?
' No, while I breathe, shall England lead the van
' With swift successions of her bright array,
' For 'tis the latest exploit crowns the man,
' And we, honour compels, must end as we began.

[1] There is no question but that Sir John Barrow, a man of science,
a learned geographer, and an enthusiastic patriot, was the chief pro-
moter of all enterprises in the way of discovery—especially, as became
the Secretary of the Admiralty, of maritime ones. He again and
again urged the prosecution of the search for the north-west passage,
and entered heart and soul into the objects of the Franklin expedition.   In no other month, therefore, could I have more fittingly
placed both the arguments for that expedition and an eloquent appeal
on its behalf.   It seems to me that I am also thus best able to promote
the development of the poem.

XXII

'To state what daily knowledge I have stored,[1]
'Me it beseems not, adding bit to bit,
'Nor how o'er endless charts these eyes have pored,
'(Each nature boasts its equal labours fit) ;
'Still to the Pole my earnest fancies flit,
'As longing to behold a drama's end ;
'Such deep desires within my bosom sit,
'To latest times our country's fame to send,
'And linked with her high name fair science to extend.

XXIII

'Deem not her service suits ignoble souls,
'Nor count that quiet spoils less splendid are
'Than triumphs won where battle's thunder rolls ;
'Not solely honour is the right of war ;
'Nor wounds, nor maimed limb, nor valour's scar,
'Tho' glorious, danger symbolise alone,—
'Milder, not less eternal, shines their star,
'Their path with perils fresh and thick is strown,
'Who, toiling day and night, search lands and seas
    unknown.

[1] Besides 'Lives of Lords Macartney, Anson, and Howe,' 'An Account of the Mutiny of the Bounty,' 'Travels in South Africa' (2 vols. 4to), and 'Travels in China and Cochin China' (2 vols. 4to), Sir John Barrow's articles in the 'Quarterly Review' alone, nearly 200 in number, fill, bound up, 12 separate vols. Amongst them many, and perhaps the most interesting, relate to the Arctic seas and Polar expeditions: he also wrote several articles in the 'Encyclopædia Britannica,' and prepared for the press numberless MSS. of travellers in all parts of the globe. He was also the founder of the Royal Geographical Society.

XXIV

' Full well ye know how round the mighty world,
' Tossed on all seas, brave British barques have sped,
' And everywhere old England's flag unfurled,
' Detecting now what isles in ocean's bed
' Remotely lie, or now their sails outspread
' Tow'rds either pole, and oceans ice-compressed :
' One work remains yet unaccomplishèd,
' This polar Asian path by north and west ;
' Till Britain it unveil, I little sleep or rest.

XXV

' Near thrice ten years adventurous have rolled,
' Since Ross and Parry broke inaction's spell,[1]
' Since Buchan sailed with Franklin,[1] comrades bold ;
' No danger could those splendid spirits quell,
' No tale of wonder theirs exceeds to tell ;
' And many a voyager since then has found,
' Sailing with th' op'ning leaf, and when it fell,
' Homeward returning, channel, bay, and sound,
' Or traced the trending coast, and mapped its tortuous
    bound.

XXVI

' Much have we learned, much still remains to learn,
' Not all at once does Nature lift her veil,
' Not one bold stroke may the grand triumph earn,
' But toil gigantic, hearts that never quail,
' And patience, that ne'er knows what 'tis to fail,
' Shall rend its secret from the pole at last,
' Tho' cased in adamant and locked in mail,
' Tho' wildest winter rage around the mast
' Hissing with arrowy sleet, roaring with horrid blast.

[1] In the year 1818.

XXVII

'I know who scoff th' adventure, say I dream,
'Compute the endless labour, danger great,
'While small the uses and uncertain seem:
'But ye shall judge if they or I most prate;
'For grant in Arctic seas no watery gate
'To Asia's shores, or one no ship may pass,
'Yet who without th' attempt the truth can state?
'Still round the pole is moved a sea of glass;
'Madly we reason else, tho' much a frozen mass.[1]

XXVIII

'How otherwise, if no connexion be,
'From Behring's distant straits beyond the pole,
'Between Atlantic and Pacific sea,
'Should tides in Hudson's bay so swiftly roll,
'Then too most high sweeping their land-locked goal,
'When from north-west the gusty breezes blow?
'Add too the current setting from the pole,
'On which huge icebergs ride, and drift-logs flow,
'Torn from their isthmus home south of far Mexico.

[1] Not to distract the reader's attention by too frequent notes, I will here say, once for all, that the scientific arguments put into Barrow's mouth in the next two stanzas have been condensed from different writers, but chiefly from Scoresby's 'Arctic Regions.' Any-one who wants to be more fully acquainted with the *pros* and *cons* on this subject, would do well to read Chapter I. Sect. III. of that very interesting work. The edition possessed by me is that of 1820, two vols. published by Constable, Edinburgh. I do not know whether there is a later one.

XXIX

'Have we not heard how the harpoonèd whale,
'Bearing the angry weapon in its back,
'Lashing the billows with its frenzied tail,
'And madly rushing on an alien track,
'Spitzbergen's native seas and icy pack   .
'Deserted, seeks in Davis' straits a home,
'Borne round the pole ? traced skins, that rude hands
       tack
'Of Indians or Esquimaux, who roam,
'Sketch the lands north and west all washed with freez-
       ing foam.

XXX

'Yet, if no path exist, or locked in ice,
'And nature interpose dread forms uncouth,
'Not less a thousand deeds of enterprise
'Invite, and multifarious claims of truth;
  Tho' much is won by time, much ardent youth
'Shall win and vig'rous manhood ; virgin ground
'Remains, remains America forsooth,
'From east to west along its northern bound
'Seldom that echo'd yet to European sound.

XXXI

'Doth any ask how soon and when to sail ?
'No time to me seems like the present hour :
'As lustrous gold surpasses silver pale,
'To-day excels to-morrow's waning power,
'And dull delay was e'er mischance's dower ;—
'To-day, with hearts framed for a mighty need,
'England's heroic tars, the prime and flower,
'Expect the conquest of a splendid deed,
'Ready to follow swift where bravest captain lead.

XXXII

' Now favourably too events conspire
' For our success : behold the gallant ships
' Returned from the Antarctic tempest dire,
' Erebus and Terror ; none their fame eclipse,
' And oft their tale shall start to seamen's lips ;
' What better prows to face the Arctic breeze ?
' Nay, while each keel with southern seaweed drips,
' Keen let us haste, the swift occasion seize,
' Refit them for the north, nor suffer hateful ease.[1]

XXXIII

' But lately too have Dease and Simpson traced
' What Franklin or what Back left unexplored,
' Down rapids whirled, almost by death embraced,
' Till gained at last the sea around them roared
' With wind and ice ; they from a height that soared
' Aloft in air beheld gulfs, straits, and isles
' On ev'ry side ; then re-embarked on board,
' Mapped two successive years three hundred miles,
' With patience unexcelled, and superhuman toils.[2]

[1] The Erebus and Terror returned from their expedition to the Antarctic ocean in September, 1843, having been absent from England exactly four years, and having spent three winters near the south pole.   An interesting account of the expedition was published by Sir James C. Ross, who was the commander of it, in 1847.   To Sir James Ross, one of our greatest living navigators, amongst many other successful results of his expeditions to either pole, we owe the discovery of both magnetic poles.

[2] In 1837–9 Mr. Thomas Simpson and Mr. Peter W. Dease, officers of the Hudson's Bay Company, discovered and traced, after descending the Mackenzie river to the coast, about 300 miles of Arctic shore previously unexplored.   To accomplish this result they traversed in boats more than 1600 miles of polar sea.

XXXIV

'Since then th' eventful years such harvest yield,
'Fraught with less danger, surer of success
'Our aim becomes, for narrowed is the field
'Of strict research, o'er which we still must press,
'Nor much left vaguely, as at first, to guess ;[1]
'Shame were it now our fervour to abate,
'When too of old men ran such risks for less,
'The best examples of heroic fate ;
'A few of many more succinct I will relate.

XXXV

'I pass if e'er fictitious Argo sailed,
'But still his ship of mocking stars the sport,
'These pale-faced shores the safe Himilco hailed ;[2]
'Whom Pytheas loosed from the Phocœan port[3]
'Bolder outstript, nor turned his prow till caught
'By inexperienced fog and blasts unchained
'Off furthest Orkneys, when the night is short,
'And sun scarce sets, then icy mists were rained,
'And back he deeming hied the world's last verge
    attained.

[1] So indeed then it seemed, such enormous additions having been made to our geographical knowledge of the countries subjacent to the pole since the year 1818, by Parry's, Beechey's, and John Ross's voyages, and the land expeditions of Franklin, Back, Dease, and Simpson. Yet before the north-west passage could be discovered, as much remained to be done, and the intricate configuration of the coasts had to be slowly unravelled.

[2] Himilco, the Carthaginian, coasted Spain and France, and afterwards advanced as far as the southern shores of Britain.

[3] Pytheas, a native of Marseilles, a little later than Himilco, about the time of Alexander the Great, is said to have sailed as far as Iceland, but to have been repelled by a strange kind of fog, which he describes as 'neither earth, air, nor sky, but a mixture of all three.'

XXXVI

' Who has not heard how the historic sire,[1]
' Halicarnassus' son, bound by the spell
' Of knowledge, posts with feet that never tire,
' All secrets of all lands to learn and tell,
' Waste Scythia's snows, the sun-reflecting well?
' Not less of kings proud fame records the tales
' That Necho's, Philadelphus' glories swell;[2]
' Thro' arid sands this hewed his huge canals,
' Round Afric's southmost coast that sped his flying
    sails.

---

[1] For the benefit of such readers as have not been able to study the classics (and I hope that my poem may be popular enough to have many such), I beg leave to say that ' the historic sire' is Herodotus, and that ' the sun-reflecting well' in line 5 is the well of Syene in south Egypt. The latitude of this place, 24° 5′ 23″, was an object of interest to the ancient geographers. They thought it seated directly under the tropic, and that on the day of the summer solstice a vertical staff cast no shadow, and the sun's disc was reflected in a well at noonday. As the ancients were not acquainted with the true tropic, this statement is incorrect, though not far from the truth.

[2] Necho succeeded Psammetichus as king of Egypt in 617 B.C., and was a man of great energy. He commenced a vast canal to join the Nile with the Arabian gulf; but, according to Herodotus, desisted from the enterprise, warned by an oracle that the profit of it would be only for barbarian invaders. But his memory is preserved to us by the circumnavigation of Africa by the Phœnicians whom he sent for that purpose. This they did in little more than two years, setting out by the Arabian gulf, and returning through the straits of Gibraltar.

Ptolemy Philadelphus, second king of Egypt of the race of Ptolemies, pursued scientific studies with great keenness, cut canals, founded many colonies, and raised Egypt to great power and wealth.

XXXVII

' Then came the Norsemen of succeeding time,[1]
' Nadodd, Ohthere, Eirek, and Biarni,
' Spontaneous emigrants in manhood's prime,
' Each leader of a swarming colony ;—
' O'er waves unmapped, beneath th' inconstant sky,
' Perfidious stars their guides, in clumsy barque
' Tumultuous wind and sea they did defy,
' Three hundred years ere yet o'er billows dark
'Columbus' straining eyes the long-hoped cont'nent mark.

XXXVIII

' To whom unknown the tale of Barentz old?[2]
' From Holland, freed from bigot yoke of Spain,
' He twice his sails audacious did unfold,
' And drove his keels along thro' frosted main
' Past Misery's mount in water's narrow lane
' To farthest Nova Zembla bleak and clear ;
' There wintry blasts the starving men detain,
' Nor Barentz saw again his country dear,
' But dying takes the chart and points the course to steer.

[1] The deeds of the bold Scandinavian Vikings, who, in frail open barques, with none of the contrivances and resources of science, and no geographical knowledge, yet discovered and colonised Iceland and Greenland, and one of whom, the pirate Biarni, is said even to have penetrated to the American mainland, are full of interest to a maritime nation like the English, and may fairly demand a fleeting notice here.

[2] If anyone wishes to read a graphic account of Barentz's voyage, and his very heroic death, he will find such in ' Voyages and Discoveries in the Arctic Regions,' No. 73 of Longman's ' Traveller's Library.'

XXXIX

'Such deeds of daring e'en of old were done,
'Shall wealthy time's last heirs do less then they ?
'Or less than those who sailed the frozen zone,
'What time the youthful Tudor dying lay,
'Our countrymen ?[1] fate barred their homeward way,
'Alas ! or pair of luckless Portuguese,
'The brothers Cortereal,[2] who sailed astray,
'First one and then the other ? rather the breeze
'Waft us that sped of old th' immortal Genoese.

XL

'Not less our aim, nor less demanding faith,
'He sailed the long-hoped continent to find,
'He sailed and found ; we sail to find the path,
'Which found more closely knits all human kind,
'And nearer draws Eastern to Western mind ;
'High is their task and noble their renown
'By land and sea, the pioneers combined,
'Who strive, old barriers rending, to enthrone
'Humanity, and make our common nature known.

[1] The unfortunate expedition of Sir Hugh Willoughby, which set sail May 10, 1553.

[2] Gaspar and Miguel Cortereal, two brothers of a noble Portuguese house, were amongst the earliest who sailed in quest of a north-west passage. Gaspar in his final voyage was overtaken by a fearful storm in Frobisher's strait, and perished in it. His brother Miguel set out to seek for him, but never returned, uncertainty still veiling his actual fate. To a third brother, anxious to embark after the other two, the Portuguese king refused permission to go. The father of these three, John Vaz Cortereal, was also a heroic navigator, and is thought by some to have forestalled our Cabot in the discovery of Newfoundland.

XLI

' What more to waveworn tars need now be said,
' To whom the rolling sea is as a wife,
' The tossing billows smoother than a bed,
' The ship a home, and their still sweetest life
'The charm of action and the joy of strife,
'Whether o'er tropic blue their way they urge,
' Or far Antarctic flout with perils rife,
' Whose frost-locked waters girdle the world's verge,
' Now bound in icy mail, now freshly loosed in surge?

XLII

' All thro' the year, in belted blanket dressed,
' O'er frosted wave 'neath clouded skies or clear,
' The trader speeds with ardour unrepressed,
' And still halloes his dogs with hearty cheer;
' Nor blinding snows, nor biting blasts severe,
' Nor tangled glens delay; still on he drives,
' Till to some Indian lodge his sledge draws near;
' There soon in sight the dusky band arrives,
' With whom he deals for fur and bargain hard contrives.

XLIII

' All seasons persevering fishers sail
' In strong-ribbed hulls defying wind and sea,
' And spear the seal, or fire the diving whale ;—[1]
' Surprised it darts, and struggling to be free
' This way and that escapes convulsively,
' Striking with head and fins and tail flung wide ;
' Deep in its back th' incessant enemy
' Plunges harpoon and lance ; on ev'ry side
' Jets out the vital shower—boats, men, ice, waves are
        dyed.[2]

For notes ([1]) and ([2]) see next page.

XLIV

' What then for furs shall trader speed alone
' O'er trackless wastes, or after whale and seal
' The fisher sole approach the frozen zone,
' Nor we, far higher enterprise, reveal
' What still the jealous ice-barred straits conceal,
' Leave the last links along the Arctic shore
' Unsought, unfound, unjoined, let others steal
' The old renown and glory once we wore,
' By Hearne, Mackenzie won, the famous pair of yore ?[3]

---

[1] ' The harpoon is thrown from the hand, or fired from a gun, the former of which, when skilfully practised, is efficient at the distance of eight or ten yards, and the latter at the distance of thirty yards or upwards. The wounded whale, in the surprise and agony of the moment, makes a convulsive effort to escape. Then is the moment of danger. The boat is subjected to the most violent blows from its head or its fins, but particularly from its ponderous tail, which sometimes sweeps the air with such tremendous fury, that both boat and men are exposed to one common destruction.'—Scoresby's ' Arctic Regions,' vol. ii. 242.

[2] Scoresby describes with equal vividness the whale's final death, the incessant plunging of harpoons and lances aimed at its vitals, its exhaustion, and the discharge of blood with air and mucus from its blow-holes. I quote his last sentence. ' The sea, to a great extent around, is dyed with its blood, and the ice, boats, and men are sometimes drenched with the same.'—Vol. ii. 248.

[3] Hearne, employed by the Hudson Bay Company to explore the north-west coast of America (1769–1772), was the first European that succeeded in reaching the Arctic ocean. Mr. (afterwards Sir Alexander) Mackenzie traced the river which now bears his name to its junction with the sea.

XLV

' Shall danger be our bugbear, dread of toil,
' Whose names are British, borne by British sires ?
' What ! do our torpid veins forget to boil,
' Slack are the nerves, slumber the antique fires ?
' Away false thoughts, soft ease, and dull desires :
' We still must be whate'er our fathers were,
' What all the men whose glory never tires,
' Davis, and Hudson, Baffin, Frobisher,
' Knight, Waymouth, Cook, and Phipps, names bright as
    starry sphere.

XLVI

' Shall later nations snatch the crown away,
' Her palm to novices our country yield,
' Contented with forgotten yesterday,
' And, which we sowed, shall others reap the field ? '
  So spoke the man, of Britain's fame the shield,
  Whose tones th' assembled sailor-chivalry
  Drank with one ear, then loud the clamour pealed
  Of men marine, and smote the vaulted sky,
Whilst in that ardent throng glowed ev'ry kindling eye.

XLVII

  With proofs confirmative, and minds as keen,
  Parry, the Rosses, Richardson, Back, King,
  Beaufort and Sabine, most of whom had been
  Sailors themselves within the Arctic ring,
  To Barrow's views authoritative cling ;
  Well-weighed opinion Franklin adds, and store
  Of long experience, ends by offering
  Himself to lead, tho' verging on threescore,
No work so near his heart, no prize he sighed for more.

XLVIII

Whom thus the good Lord Haddington bespoke :—
' Franklin, thy soul what zealous duty fires
' I know, thy heart I know of British oak,
' But aging limbs incessant labour tires
' At last, and nerves, our life's electric wires,
' Droop slack; thy sixty years just end assign
' To toil, rest thee 'midst England's honoured sires,
   Thyself most honoured.' Him with eyes that shine,
Brief answer made the knight, ' I am but fifty-nine.'[1]

XLIX

Nor more he said: but when those words were heard,
So resolutely grand, sublimely few,
'Twas felt on him alone could be conferred
The post of honour, he must lead the crew,
And with his spirit ev'ry man imbue ;
With such a captain half the work seemed done
Ere well commenced, and soon the tidings flew
   That sailing preparations were begun,
That Franklin would be off ere June's first rising sun.

---

[1] ' It was at one time intended that Fitzjames (whose genius and energy marked him as no ordinary officer) should command the expedition ; but just at this time ' (1845) ' Sir John Franklin was heard to say that he considered the post to be his birth-right as the senior Arctic explorer in England.' . . . . ' Lord Haddington, then First Lord, with that kindness which ever distinguished him, suggested that Franklin might well rest at home on his laurels. ' I might find a good excuse for not letting you go, Sir John,' said the Peer, ' in the tell-tale record which informs me that you are sixty years of age.' ' No, no, my Lord,' was Franklin's rejoinder, ' I am only fifty-nine.' Before such earnestness all scruples yielded, the offer was officially made and accepted, to Sir John Franklin was confided the Arctic expedition, &c., &c.'—Captain S. Osborn's ' Career, &c. of Franklin,' pp. 34, 35.

L

So swift of soul he was, mature of mind,
Of fiery purpose, fitted to command,
And well he knew what his keen wit designed
Instant to follow with unerring hand;
Now long his fame had spread throughout the land,
As one by hardships braced, and perils tried,
The proper leader of heroic band,
And volunteers flocked gladly to his side,
To do or die with him, let weal or woe betide.

LI

Blithely they stepped from many an English home,
Leaving the lowly cot, the lordly house,
Charmed with the prospect of the tumbling foam;
Farewell they said to father, mother, spouse,
Or soothed with oft-reiterated vows
One dearer yet, and laughed her fears away,
And dried the drops beneath her pensive brows,
Dissembling the sad hours with bearing gay,
Then tore themselves apart, unmanned by further stay.

LII

Ah me! thrice sev'n the full-leaved Junes have fled,
And thrice the seventh moon for hunters burns,
Since those brave hearts their latest farewell said,
Nor, since they sailed, one single soul returns,—
But weeping Mem'ry bends o'er empty urns:—
Then with high hopes and happy auguries
They went, nor aught of cloud their joy discerns,
But as sunshiny waves to azure skies,
So danced to mirthsome mood their pleasure-sparkling
    eyes.

LIII

Oh! for a rush of song! a voice divine!
Oh! for a Homer's thrilling tones of fire,
A Virgil's graceful art and stately line!
Oh! for a master hand to strike the lyre!
Me from th' unequal task fain to retire
Shame checks, and noble hope to tell the tale,
If better muse a fitter bard inspire,
Happily vanquished, yet lest none prevail,
Soaring on wing too bold, breasting a jealous gale.

LIV

And Thou—whate'er thy name, of heav'nly power,
No tenant now of the harmonious hill,
Reft of Ilissus and thy Attic bower,
Nor yet by Tiber's side or Arno's rill,
Spirit of poesy, assist me still,—
For still thou breath'st immortal; oh! awake!
To wingèd words add sweet melodious skill,
Sweep thro' the chords and lofty music make
To thoughts that stir the blood, and inmost nature shake.

LV

Glad would I pause and cite each one by name,
Recording those departed souls sublime,
Who, at the call of duty and of fame,
Left home and dearest ties in life's gay prime
To woo the terrors of the icy clime;
Ah me! renown shall gild them, like a sun,
For aye remembered to the latest time,
All now with splendid brows and glory won,
From earth's fair fields of light to death's dark absence
    gone.

LVI

Each would I sing of the devoted crew,
But that so long the track before me lies;
Twice seventy there sailed in all save two,
Too many to be spared, too dear a prize
Almost for honour's immortalities,
Tho' them her clear-voiced clarion proclaims
Where from the wave remotest islands rise,
And triply rings aloud the leaders' names,
Franklin, the vet'ran knight, brave Crozier, frank
　　　Fitzjames.

LVII

Crozier the captain of the Terror sails,
Crozier all toils with Parry shared of old;
Scarce Franklin's self recounts so stirring tales,
Escapes more hair-breadth, or adventures bold,
As Crozier brave can modestly unfold;
He too with younger Ross renown had earned
In dreary deserts of austerest cold,
Braving th' Antarctic, whence but just returned
He posts to Franklin's side, such ardour in him burned.

LVIII

Second on board the Erebus, Fitzjames,
And next to Franklin, fired with gen'rous zeal,
Anticipates and backs his leader's aims,
Catching the kindred spark, flint struck by steel;
His eager soul his glowing eyes reveal;
High hopes are his, but knowledge calms his brow,
And patient labour for the common weal;
To him magnetic observations now
Franklin entrusts, well skilled why needles veer to show.

LIX

With these sailed Fairholme, Hodgson, Graham Gore,
Vescomte, Des Vaux, Stanley, Goodsir and Reid,
Peddie, Macdonald, many brave men more,
Quick, resolute, prompt for a nation's need,
For whose dear loss long, England, must thou bleed,
Nurse the deep wound, and feel sharp sorrow's stings,
Tho' ev'ry year from like heroic seed
A crop as brave to fill the gap upsprings,
And rules the waves, ocean's hereditary kings.

LX

The rest were seamen, weather-beaten tars,
Choice hardy messmates of the proper sort,
Light-limbed to climb the masts and clear the spars,[1]
Not such as you pick up in any port,
But seasoned with experience dear-bought
In frequent voyages on ev'ry sea,
Where often they had been rough Neptune's sport;
Now glad were they with such a chief to be,
And did whate'er he bade with swift alacrity.

LXI

Nor ye depart unsung, historic two!
Hail! Erebus and Terror, dauntless pair,
Twin stars of fame, for ever fresh and new,
Hard were the buffets ye before did bear
Thro' bergs terrific steered with nicest care
In the bleak southern circumpolar waste;—
Daring discoverers, receive the share
Of poet's praise, ere yet again ye haste
To lose old England's cliffs o'er billows tossed and chased.

---

[1] 'The men were fine hearty sailors, mostly from the northern sea-ports.'—Captain S. Osborn's 'Narrative,' p. 37.

LXII

Three years' provisions in each ship are stored,—
Three years, 'tis hoped, will bring them safely back;
And all that arts inventive can afford,
Food, implements, ice-saws, crow's-nest they pack,
The crow's-nest reared on high above the wrack
Of nature, on the dizzy topmost mast,
A barrel lined with canvas or with sack,
To scoff the pelting snows and biting blast,
In this th' ice-master sits and cons the prospect vast.

LXIII

Now, while with preparations still detained,
The busy captains know no idle hour,
But o'er the chart with eyes intently strained,
And gifted with their predecessor's dower
Of rich experience, a guiding power,
Shape their intended route, and wisely plan
Thro' gulf and strait from icy shore to shore
The predetermined course as best they can,
And with prospective wit all circumstances scan.

LXIV

Of all the lands beneath the polar sky
To him that westward sails from Baffin's bay
There is an isle that central seems to lie,
Marking to Behring's straits the onward way,
'Russell' its name, familiar as the day
To English ears; Cape Walker bluff and bleak
Guards its north-eastern side, seen far away
By tars emerged from Barrow's straits, who seek
With rapid-hailing eyes its lofty-looming peak.

LXV

Thither swift Parry first with prosp'rous gale
Had winged his flight, and others with less toil
Since then had followed his advent'rous sail,
Passing on either side a barren soil
Rockbound, though there no glaciers creep and coil ;[1]
Thither was Franklin bent at once to steer,
Hoping thence south and west, without a foil,
To reach Pacific waves o'er waters clear,
Nor knew what icy bars, what currents interfere.

LXVI

Yet as a man with many shifts prepared,
If one should fail, not lost, but prompt to try
The next, and then the next, leaves nothing spared
By which to gain his end eventually,
So was he bent another course to ply,
Should frost beyond Cape Walker drive him back,
And up the sound of Wellington to hie,
Whose sunlit waves dance free from icy pack,[2]
Thence round the Parry isles a north-west passage track.

[1] The absence of glaciers from the coast of North Devon, a coast in this respect so different from that of Greenland, which is remarkable for their abundance, is specially noted by Captain Osborn in his ' Career, &c. of Sir J. Franklin,' p. 42.

[2] Wellington Channel is remarkable for its comparative freedom from ice. Captain Osborn (p. 43) thus writes of it: ' Wellington Channel is open, and smiles and sparkles in blue and sunlit waves, as if luring them to the north-west.'

LXVII

If there too spiteful winter closed the gate,
Debarred both routes, still all the south remained,
Thro' Regent inlet or James Ross's strait
By which the continent could be attained,
Thence coasting westwards might a path be gained,
Slow, toilsome, tortuous to the longed-for goal
Beyond the river with its copper stained,
Rolling its umber water tow'rds the pole,
Well Franklin kenned those parts, twice had he traced
    the whole.[1]

[1] 'According to Sir John Richardson, who was on intimate terms with Sir John Franklin, his plans were to shape his course in the first instance for the neighbourhood of Cape Walker, and to push to the westward in that parallel; or, if that could not be accomplished, to make his way southwards, to the channel discovered on the north coast of the continent, and so on to Behring's Straits; failing success in that quarter, he meant to retrace his course to Wellington Sound, and attempt a passage northwards of Parry's Islands, and if foiled there also, to descend Regent Inlet, and seek the passage along the coast discovered by Messrs. Dease and Simpson.'—Simmonds' 'Arctic Regions,' p. 153.

There is no doubt that Franklin's plans were as above described, and in 1845 Cape Walker would certainly seem the most desirable point d'appui to be first attained for reconnoitring their route onwards. At that time, and not indeed till the return of McClure in 1854, very little comparatively was known of the relative amount of sea and land west, north-west, and south-west of Melville Sound, and almost nothing of that vast accumulation of ice beyond Bank's Land westwards, which inflicted such damage on the ships of McClure and Collinson, and would probably always prove the most invincible obstacle to a north-west passage. Franklin, it seems, could not get beyond Cape Walker, owing to ice; he therefore sailed up Wellington Channel on to Hamilton Island and Penny's Strait, but compelled by the ice again turned southward, and spent his first winter at Beechey Island. But in this remarkably successful voyage he had explored *three hundred miles* of previously unknown channels, and first found the water-passage existing between Cornwallis and Bathurst islands.

LXVIII

So now, his future all securely planned,
The veteran chafes at any more delay,
And, both his ships equipped and fully manned,
Longs to be gone with summer's earliest ray ;
Nor Crozier nor Fitzjames desired to stay,—
Such zeal in them their leader's fire begot,
Such great enthusiasm inspired that day,
Such cloudless joy without a speck or spot
Beguiled the men, as if each drew a happy lot.

LXIX

But I, scarce ready to dismiss them yet
Into the dark across the fleeting wave,
The days, the hours, last ling'ring moments wet
With tearful love's fond drops would gladly save,
Fain would delay, still weaving o'er the brave
Fresh wreaths of song, as one that stays to catch
The sun's last beam half hid in ocean grave,
And watching still prolongs his pensive watch,
Snatching a farewell gaze, still farewell turns to snatch.

LXX

How sweet the music of the flowing tide,
Ripple on ripple stealing peacefully
O'er the smooth sandy bed, which now they hide,
Whilst all the air is still, and not a sigh
Of wind escapes to make a lullaby ;
But one lone flake above sails flushed with pink,
The sun's last gift, escaping tranquilly
Beneath the wave from airy clouds that drink
His rays, but soon themselves must fade, and melt, and
    sink.

LXXI

The golden radiance dies from leaf and bough,
And unreflected in the lake's clear glass
Against the skies the trees rise larger now,
Sleeping with folded branch, an unstirred mass,
And cast a doubtful shadow o'er the grass ;
Nor sheep, nor cattle, singly, may be seen
By wayfarers belated as they pass,
For swift on-coming night hides all the green,
Concludes laborious day, and shuts the living scene.

LXXII

Then darkness curtains nature with a pall,
Light in her rainbow-coloured mantle flies,
And undistinguished blackness covers all ;
Only perchance beneath the scarce-seen skies
Dim cliffs loom vast in vague immensities,
While shines or seems to shine the random star,
And sweet forgetful sleep seals wearied eyes,
But, soon as Sol remounts his amber car,
The dear familiar morn shows all things as they are.

LXXIII

But no familiar morn restores the crew
Once rocked upon the sea's uneasy bed,
So many setting suns they sink from view,
Beyond the blank horizon's bareness fled,
No welcome hour brings back each precious head :
While thro' the glass still flits the fleeting sand,
Ere yet the anchor's weighed, the sails are spread,
Still may we see the last of that loved band,
Waiting the wind to waft them from their fatherland:—

LXXIV

The last, for never more may they behold
Fair flowers, or slender grace of waking trees,
That to the am'rous breath of spring unfold
Their dainty leaves and rustle in the breeze,
But all alone must sail the dreary seas,
Exchanging summer's prime for winter wild,
Rough labour for the sports of active ease,
And for sweet look of parent, wife, or child,
The blinding snowy plains, ice-blocks on ice-blocks piled.

LXXV

Yet rather let my lips be sealed and dumb,
Than thus forestal their doleful date of woe,
For now still round them sounds the busy hum
Of mighty London surging to and fro,
And still, as lower down the stream they go,
Familiar domes, and spires, and towers appear,
And all the sights surround, that all men know,
While now and then some ancient comrade dear
Parry, Ross, Richardson, bestows his parting cheer.

LXXVI

At Greenhithe moored the ships lie side by side,
As yet no billow rocks them, no wind blows,
Only the ebbing and the flowing tide
Of Father Thames scarce stirs them from repose;
Still, ere they leave, friend comes, and stays, and goes,
Shakes Franklin by the hand, and bids God-speed;
'Tis Saturday, and May is near its close,
Now mounts the warbling lark o'er inland mead,
Where daisies dot the grass, and cowslips hang the head.

The sacred day returns, calm, clear, and bright,
The congregated crews the deck conceal;
It is a pious, tranquillising sight,
A solemn sound to hear their voices peal
Skywards, or Franklin with deep tones that feel
Religion's charm, or brave Fitzjames aloud
Read words of holy writ, that softly steal
Into the sailors' hearts, and chase the crowd
Of troublous thoughts afar, as rays dispel the cloud.[1]

---

[1] For the account here given of the last days spent in England by the crews of the Erebus and Terror, I am most indebted to the kindness of Miss Cracroft, the niece of Sir John Franklin, and the constant companion of Lady Franklin. From her letter, admirable in its minute particulars, as ladies' letters are wont to be, I quote the following extract: 'With respect to the departure of the Erebus and Terror, it is more easy to answer your direct questions than to describe the scene at Greenhithe. It was on Monday, May 19, following a quiet Sunday, on which day my dear uncle read the Morning Service to the assembled officers and crew of the Erebus, Captain Fitzjames taking the Lessons. Such a service was sure to be made doubly impressive by the devotion (habitual to him) of my uncle's manner of conducting it.

'The afternoon was occupied on board in writing final letters, and making last arrangements of books, &c. We then all went ashore again (my aunt had come down on the Saturday to Greenhithe), and about 8 o'clock on Monday morning my dear uncle left us. The day was fair, if not brilliant, and by 10 or 11 o'clock the Erebus and Terror, with the Baretto Junior store-ship, were in tow of the Rattler and another small steamer, gliding down the river (as we watched them first from the pier and afterwards from a hill above) without show or indication of the mission to which they were destined.

'My uncle's friends had previously taken leave of him—Parry, Richardson (who had just lost his wife—my uncle's niece, and my first cousin), James Ross, Sabine, Mr. Robert Brown, and many many others, some in town, some on board at Woolwich, before the ships dropped down to Greenhithe.'

LXXVIII

The noon, their last ere England's shores are left,
Flows on with busy packing occupied,
Or final letters to their friends bereft
Of consolation full and joyous pride
They write, and tell how with to-morrow's tide
The Erebus and Terror anchors weigh,
And seaward borne along the river glide,
A few upon the shore yet rambling stray
Till nightfall, then embark, so ends their latest day.

LXXIX

'Tis morning; Franklin, last upon the strand,
Parts from his friends, parts from his consort dear,
And hails the ship, swept from his native land,
While still affection's voice and words that cheer
Sustain his soul and ring within his ear :
Beneath the gunwale of the vessel now
The boat is moored, and now the space is clear,
Upon the deck he stands with tranquil brow,
And gives the order prompt, 'up anchors, steamers tow.'

LXXX

Glows the whole crew with bustling promptitude,
And soon the anchor's ponderous teeth suspends,
Still while the voyage from the shore is viewed,
And still the gazing crowd of loving friends
Commencement of the enterprise attends,
Two steamers forwards drag the destined pair ;—
The pier recedes, the hill that high ascends
Above the pier is lost in distant air,
On to Sheerness they glide with sunny hours and fair.

LXXXI

What burning hope fires each adventurous breast,
What zeal the long-hoped north-west track to find
And set on endless toil the crown and crest,
And on their brows a noble wreath to bind.
Tho' many men they sail, yet one their mind;
So free from pomp, so quietly they pass,
You would not guess the part to them assigned,
What glorious palm awaits, what woes, alas!
Nor fear but placid cruise on summer sea of glass.

LXXXII

England, proud mother of heroic men,
Long mayst thou nurse such children to such aims,
Not less thy striplings manly virtue ken
Than the crowned victors of Olympian games,
Severely schooled, shunning whatever shames,
To serve the state and love the common weal;
What tho' no tourney, seen of lovely dames,
Inspire their souls to couch the shining steel,
A wider field is theirs, their praise the public peal.

LXXXIII

Theirs the arena of free rights, free birth,
Theirs just ambition's hope, the common lot,
Whose prizes only fall to native worth,
Or by devotion's faithful toil are got;
But let him be taintless of sordid spot,
Who thee would serve, my country, let him be,
Like knight of old, exempt of selfish blot,
Whoe'er in court, or camp, aspiringly
Thee serves, or civic hall, a guardian of the free.

LXXXIV

Such was our Palmerston, mourned yesterday,
Mourned now, the last great statesman taken hence,
Whose years of work ne'er made the heart less gay,
English his soul, his pleasant eloquence
Was home-spun wit and sparkling common-sense :
Oh! fresh brave oak green amid wintry snows,
Oh! young old man of rich experience,
Thy sun is set, thou saw'st an era close,
Now sleep thee sound where all our worthiest repose.[1]

LXXXV

Such too were they, that high devoted band,
Who now down Thames have gone and sailèd are.
Brighter than wreath that e'er Greek's temple spanned,
Olive or parsley, shines thy praise's star,
My country, guiding them thro' wat'ry war,
Nor seeks their leader any other fame
Than that his crest should be without a bar,
And that thro' life he might endure the same,
Dangers o'ercoming old, as he in youth o'ercame.

---

[1] Let it not be thought out of place that I here introduce a stanza to the memory of Lord Palmerston. Anxious at home to promote the happiness of all classes of his countrymen, the encourager abroad of constitutional freedom throughout the world, a steadfast friend, a genial and generous foe, cosmopolite in his sympathies, but an English citizen, Lord Palmerston devoted a long life to his country's service, and, not seeking the first place, obtained it, as confessedly the fittest. As a true exemplar of an English gentleman, a few lines here are not irrelevant; but, if his death be considered, they are the more appropriate, for surely the sage of old, severely regarding all the circumstances of man's life, but most his final close, would have pronounced him truly happy.

LXXXVI

Now from old Thames' winding wave emerged,
Steamers dismissed and crowded canvas set,
Northwards past Essex coast their prows are urged,
And as upon their way they hourly get,
By home-bound ships still in the offing met,
One after one, receding counties hide,
Suffolk and Norfolk first, then dearer yet
His well-known sands of native Lincoln glide
From Franklin's eyes, where his loved parents lived and
  died.

LXXXVII

Yorkshire's long shores all stretching to the north,
And Scarb'ro's castled cliff, the sea-gulls' post,
Far fades, Northumberland, and Frith of Forth,
Aberbrothok, and Aberdeen are lost,
More to the west they steer, glad to have crossed
Fierce Pentland's ever restless sea of foam,
By rough gusts swept and tidal eddies tossed;
Briefly they make Pomona's isle their home,
Whose misty headlands watch th' Atlantic billows come.

LXXXVIII

There is a cone-shaped hill that fronts the sea,[1]
Secluded Stromness nestling lies below,
Hoar ocean's desolate immensity
Hence may you view, and little else, I trow,
Here may you hear the gathering tempest grow,
Gales roar, hoarse breakers burst, shrill sea-fowl
  scream,
Nor softer strains those windy summits know,
But stormy concerts heard in twilight gleam
Rock best the sailor's brain, and make his sweetest dream.

---

[1] 'Above the town of Stromness rises a conical-shaped hill; it has,

LXXXIX

The spot is sacred, a memorial crest,
For hither mess-mates came from either crew,
And this, they say, was the last spot they pressed,
'Twas here they stood, and took their latest view,
Ere Franklin re-embarked, prompt to renew
His western voyage o'er the wat'ry waste,
With the unsetting sun; full well he knew
That during summer must he speed with haste,
Too soon would frost return and waves in ice be cased.

XC

Away they sail, and sight again the land,
No longer British, wondrous to behold,
Greenland's south coast, whose pillared peaks upstand
Guarding the clustered islets, bleak and cold,
That sleep beneath, mountains behind are rolled
Lofty and loftier against the sky,
Their snowy heads the sunset clouds enfold,
Or float around them rich with ev'ry dye,
Far off, in distance dim, the misty glaciers lie.[1]

I believe, been immortalised by Scott, in his "Pirate;" it had yet
deeper interest for me, for I was told that up it had toiled dear friends
now missing with Franklin. I and a kind shipmate walked out one
evening to make our pilgrimage to a spot hallowed by the visit of the
gallant and true-hearted that had gone before us; and as, amid wind
and drizzle, we scrambled up the hill, I pictured to myself how, five
short years before, those we were now in search of had done the
same. Good and gallant Gore! chivalrous Fitzjames! enterprising
Fairholme! lion-hearted Hodgson! dear Des Vaux! oh that ye knew
help was nigh!' Thus Captain S. Osborn, setting out in search of
the lost mariners, himself as enthusiastic a sailor as any, apostrophises
the noble shades of his luckless predecessors. (See his 'Arctic
Journal,' pp. 4, 5.)
    [1] For the fidelity of this description see McClintock's 'Fate of
Franklin, and his Discoveries' (pp. 17, 18), from which it is condensed.

XCI

Admiringly they gaze, nor yet delay,
But leave Cape Farewell on the starboard tack,
Steaming to Frederickshaab, first were they[1]
To front with steam the icy-rolling pack,
But steam's swift power, alas! ne'er brought them back,
Which took them swift away, and bore them then
To Disko's bay by the Whale Islands' track :
'Tis thirty days since on the open main
They spread their flying sail and first commenced their
    pain.

XCII

Their store-ship here, 'Baretto' called, departs,
Bearing such letters as the seaman writes,
Tossed on the waves to fond home-keeping hearts,
Knowing his hand hailed sweetest of delights,
And gladdest far of long-expected sights ;
The frank Fitzjames with ardour testifies
What happy concord ev'ry soul unites,
How swift their chief in all emergencies,—
And Franklin well reports, and how they still devise.[2]

---

[1] 'For the first time in Arctic annals, these discovery vessels each had auxiliary screws and engines of twenty-horse power.'—Osborn, 'Career of Franklin,' p. 36.

[2] Sir John Franklin's letter, despatched from the Whale Fish Islands, July 12, 1845, will be found in Simmonds' 'Arctic Regions,' pp. 151, 152. Of Sir John himself, 'the warm-hearted Fitzjames writes "that Sir John was delightful; that all had become very fond of him, and that he appeared remarkable for energetic decision in an emergency. The officers were remarkable for good feeling, good humour, and great talents; whilst the men were fine hearty sailors, mostly from the northern sea-ports." Love already, it is apparent, as well as duty, bound together the gallant hearts on board the Erebus and Terror.' — Ibid.

XCIII

Not out of sight the transport vessel views[1]
The Erebus and Terror tempest-tossed
In Baffin's bay, and anxiously pursues
Her homeward route, soon from their prospect lost :
They with a calmer wave 'neath th' icebound coast
Proceed, till Cape of Sanderson is seen,
Known to the Danes and Norsemen's endless host,
Known to our whalers and discov'rers keen,
Snows o'er its crimson-threaded front of lichen lean.

XCIV

Below the giant cliffs and at their feet
Lies Upernavik, quaint and quiet town,
To wave-drenched mariner a shelter sweet,
Calm anchorage, when skies tempestuous frown,
But on to lighter skies and pools ice-strown ;—
Small wish in Franklin's heart to loiter there,
While bright mid-summer gilds the arctic zone,
His soaring mind quick wings of fancy bear
Beyond Mackenzie's waves that tow'rds the pole repair.

[1] Not wishing to encumber my poetic narrative with notes beyond what is absolutely necessary, let me say here once for all, that being anxious to follow the voyage with the minutest truth and circumstantial detail, I have availed myself to the full of Captain Osborn's admirably picturesque and graphic account. A poet, narrating facts and actual occurrences, is as dependent as a historian on others for his materials; all that can be expected of him is; that, adhering to truth, he should give those facts poetically, or omit them if that be impossible. I feel happy in being able to follow so excellent a guide as Captain Osborn, of whose very words I have as freely availed myself as Shakspeare availed himself of Plutarch's and the old chroniclers ; and Byron, in describing the shipwreck, availed himself of his grandfather's and other narratives.

XCV

For well he knew gulf, isle, and frosty creek[1]
Between Point Turnagain and Dease's strait,
And ev'ry cloud-capped and storm-battered peak
Familiarly had named, defying fate,
  And famished skies, and taming the rude hate
Of uncouth Esquimaux; in manhood's prime
Twice coasting there from morn till sunset late,
  With choice companions had he spent the time,
Escaping half alive from that inclement clime.

XCVI

Could he but reach those shores once more perforce,
All would be well and open to the west,
Toilsome and tedious but a charted course;
So on he speeds, not now the hour for rest,
  To gaze where thro' deep chasm pent and prest
The wild escaping fiord hurrying fast
Shoots like a mortal changed to spirit blest,
  And hails the sea; not e'en the glacier vast,
Moving yet motionless, detains him fleeting past.

[1] I need not here say much of the two wonderful land expeditions undertaken by Franklin, the first in the years 1819–21, the second in 1825–6. In the latter of these his whole party were only saved from being massacred by the Esquimaux through their extreme caution and prudence. In the second canto, which will treat of Franklin's earlier life, these expeditions will to some extent be described.

XCVII

Yet wondrous is the voiceless solitude
Of that strange land, the melancholy wrack
Of nature in her fierce destructive mood,
For there with lava's desolation black
Spreads inland the drear desert's footless track,
Uncrossed save by the shelter-seeking deer,
But far from thence the Esquimaux shrink back,
A dying horde, and far from thence appear
• The ruins of that race, killed by dark fate severe.[1]

XCVIII

But on thro' Melville's, on thro' Baffin's bay,
Sharp floes and tumbling masses surge around,
Whose light reflected gilds the northern day;
The south wind fails, but brighter skies are found,—
The fogs roll back, the ships advancing bound
To meet the streaming onset, from his post
The wise ice-master scans the hostile ground,
And soon selects amid the warring host
The weakest edge that lines the onward-rolling frost.

---

[1] 'Here, methought me of the mighty glacier creeping on like Time, silently yet ceaselessly; the deep and picturesque fiord pent up between precipices, huge, black, and barren; the iceberg, alone a miracle; then the great central desert of black lava and glittering ice, gloomy and unknown but to the fleet reindeer, who seeks for shelter in a region at whose horrors the hardy natives tremble; and last, but not least, the ruins of the Scandinavian inhabitants, and the present fast-disappearing race of "the Innuit" or Esquimaux.' —Captain S. Osborn's 'Arctic Journal,' p. 10.

On the uncertain fate of the Scandinavian colonisers of Greenland, see Scoresby's 'Arctic Regions,' vol. i. p. 66.

XCIX

The sails are taken in, the speed reduced,
'Steady with small helm steer,' the pilot bawls,
A whaler old to Greenland seas long used,
Then to the officer on watch he calls
To brail the after sails,[1] but fluttering falls
Each stitch of canvas, as with grinding keels
The Erebus and Terror cut the walls
Of churning ice, yielding their weight it feels,
Breaks bent beneath the bows, and round them roars and
    reels.

C

'Now with the helm hard up,' th' ice-master shouts,
Swifter they sail, to labour soon inured
Of daily conflict with the ice that floats
Their path, assaulting more the more endured ;—
Scarce any open water round is poured,
Yet still the vessels on their voyage get,
Now lugged by ropes, or now to berg secured
Lie snug awhile, the lowest that is met,
With crystal dome and spire the lofty oft upset.[2]

---

[1] 'To brail,' viz., to haul up. The noun 'brails' is explained by
Falconer in a note to his 'Shipwreck' (which poem is a perfect reper-
tory of technical sea-terms) to be 'a general name given to all the ropes
which are employed *to haul up or brail* the bottoms and lower courses
of the great sails.'

[2] Captain Osborn ('Career of Franklin,' p. 40) particularly notices
the danger of the taller icebergs, so liable to turn over, when a ship
near them would at once be crushed.

CI

Still as they sail thro' ev'ry toilsome day,
The whaling ships from Hull and Aberdeen
Hail them, and out of sight pass swift away,
But fewer now, and fewer still are seen,
Till when two months from England they have been,[1]
· The latest views the ships to iceberg moored,
Then leaves to them the solitary scene,
Meanwhile to autumn is the year restored,
Glazed shines the freezing wave with fresh ice nightly
     floored.

CII

The south wind freshens, on the vessels press,
A hundred miles of ice behind them lie,
Around them ice, in front nought else they guess,
And thro' the tempest stagger heavily;
But ' westward still,' still westward is the cry,
No time to stop whose work is but begun,
Deposit records, or raise cairns on high,
For keen their hope with the next summer's sun
Into Pacific seas thro' Behring's gates to run.

---

[1] 'For a while the discovery ships meet the whaling vessels of Aberdeen and Hull, striving, like themselves, to get through the loose ice into the waters of Pond's Bay. On July 26th (exactly sixty-five days after leaving Sheerness) 'they part company from the last of them, and pursue their solitary course alone.'—Captain S. Osborn, 'Career of Franklin,' p. 40.

'Captain Dannett, of the whaler Prince of Wales, whilst in Melville Bay, last saw the vessels of the expedition, moored to an iceberg, on July 26, in lat. 74° 48' N., long. 66° 13 W., waiting for a favourable opening through the middle ice from Baffin's Bay to Lancaster Sound.'—Simmonds' 'Arctic Regions,' p. 151.

CIII

Oh! who can tell, while the deep round them rolls,
And winds blow cold, and strangest sights surround,
What momentary doubt invades their souls?
A moment only; soon with lurch and bound
To Warrender and Hay their path is wound,
Grim capes, guarding with heads snow-silvered, steep,
On either side the portals of the sound,
Lancaster Sound, thro' which the vessels sweep,
Locked from all eyes but God's that o'er them vigils
　　　keep.

CIV

Onwards North Devon's precipices break
Against the hard blue sky, and thro' the gloom
Dark cliffs of Beechey Island rise, no flake[1]
Of snow hangs on their tops,—so steep they loom,—
Huge ebon giants,—brooding as in doom
Over the hungry plain, gaunt Famine's lair,
Spread at their feet; there in his vasty room
The haggard demon mocks his own despair,
Tearing with vulture beak the unsubstantial air.

---

[1] 'The dark and frowning cliffs of Beechey Island—cliffs too steep
for even snow-flake to hang on. There they stand, huge ebon giants,
brooding over the land of famine and suffering spread beneath their
feet.'—Captain Osborn, 'Career of Franklin,' p. 51.

CV

Bleak is North Devon, hunger's homeless home,
Valleys and plains of selfsame hue are seen,
Not e'en when summer gilds the heav'n's blue dome
They their dun robes exchange or smile in green,
A leafless land ; yet by the grim ravine,
'Neath beetling rocks or in the shallow lake,
Animal life abounds,[1] the seal serene
Basks with his shining orbs, or huge whales shake
The trembling wave, fowl feed, and walruses awake.

CVI

But here they pause not, this is not their goal,
While yet the southward-speeding sun delays,
Only with awful and admiring soul
Passing on nature's workmanship they gaze,—
What architect surpasses nature's ways ?
See frosty spires, and icy buttresses,
Like Gothic churches old, dim fronts that raise,
So Winter's hands th' eternal piles impress,
And rude rough tumbling rocks with shapely shapeless-
    ness.

[1] A fact particularly noted by Captain Osborn. 'The sterility of
the land, however, is somewhat compensated for by the plentiful
abundance of animal life upon the water. The seal, the whale, and
the walrus are there; whilst wild fowl in large flocks feed in the
calm spots under beetling cliffs, or in shallow lakes, which can be
looked down upon from the mast-head.'—p. 43.

CVII

Now are they well advanced to Walker's cape,
Whence their first plan southwards to sail and west,
And they right glad thereto their course would shape,
But that such frost-embattled foes invest,
Seen stretching far from high prospective nest ;—
But to north-west clear-sparkling waters lure,
Called from our hero-chief, who sleeps at rest ;
There Franklin, there Fitzjames haste to explore,
Better uncertain path than dull delay endure.

CVIII

So up thy channel, Wellington, they fly,
By Grinnell's land since styled, to Penny's strait,
Passing the wondrous cliffs of Majendie,
To Penny's strait, and eagerly debate
What widespread waters these which them await,
Seen from the mast-head reaching far and wide ;
With stud-sails set alow, aloft (the rate[1]
Was not so swift when first in southern tide
Victoria's cliffs they saw) the famous vessels glide.

CIX

Not there, alas ! an open sea extends,
But ice-choked waters westward stretching far ;
So back at once the gallant leader bends,
And following his swift successful star,
Finds a new path, not known to any tar,[2]
'Twixt islands from Cornwallis, Bathurst named;
So back to Barrow's straits arrived they are,
And gladly still, with spirits all untamed,
The hot chase had pursued with vessels hurt and maimed.

[1] Viz., in the expedition to the Antarctic regions, under Sir James
C. Ross, already alluded to in stanzas 32, 57, 61.

[2] 'Next, though most scantily provided with steam-power, Franklin

CX

But now chill hours return with frost and snow,
Raw whistling winds drive on the rolling floes,
A jagged phalanx, tearing as they go
Thro' Barrow's straits the fields[1] that them oppose,
And tossing fierce, while shorter, shorter grows
The dull dark day, for now the sun has fled,
Leaving the dim delightless year to close
By moon and star, as tho' the land were dead,
Whilst he, disdainful king, averts his lively head.

CXI

So short the days, so longer grow the nights,
Congeals the breath, whene'er the men respire,
And see from lip and beard, most strange of sights,
The icicle depend, till thawed by fire,—
The hearty tars laugh clad in warm attire ;
But from the starving plains and icy drouth
The ptarmigans and willow-grouse retire,
With whiter wings, and hast'ning to the south,
The flocking wild-fowl dart, and shun the land uncouth.

navigated round Cornwallis Island, which he thus proved to be an island. This last discovery of a navigable channel throughout, between Cornwallis and Bathurst Islands, though made in the very summer he left England, has remained even to this day' (Nov. 1859) 'unknown to other navigators.'—Sir R. Murchison's Preface (p. xiv.) to Captain Sir L. McClintock's ' Fate of Franklin.'

Sir Roderick Murchison in the same preface (pp. xiii. xiv.) well points out the extraordinary amount of work performed by the crews of the Erebus and Terror in this one season. ' Rarely,' as he truly says, 'has an expedition accomplished the first year more by its ships than the establishing of good winter quarters, from whence the real researches began by sledge-work in the ensuing spring.' Franklin, as before pointed out, did a great deal more than this, besides making, *en route*, very important geographical discoveries.

[1] Viz., ice-fields.

CXII

So must they seek a haven for the ships
And for themselves, and studiously beguile
The horrid time thro' winter's long eclipse;
No shelter know they near save Beechey's isle,
So thither speed, avoiding well the wile
Of drifting pack, that oft the seaman bears
Unwary and unwilling many a mile
Back to th' Atlantic; them it better fares,
Who, hauling high the keels, look well to their repairs.

CXIII

Now iron Winter rules the polar year,
Murdering light and warmth with icy hand;
Not here alternate frost and thaw appear,
But with one stroke locked springs and rivers stand
Frozen to adamant at his command;
Coldness and silence reign, and death supreme,
Snow's dazzling white encases all the land,
Nor seas nor fiords well distinguished seem,
One colour everywhere, strange as a waking dream.

CXIV

Thus far have I pursued my flight along,
Companion of their voyage well begun,
But now, embarking on another song,
Quit them awhile, by fancy strongly won
To tell what deeds by Franklin erst were done
In his heroic prime, beheld the same
Both in his rising and his setting sun;
Which finished, these again with steadfast aim
I will o'ertake and to the end record their fame.

CXV

Thus far : but homewards now I must resort,
Flying the Arctic seas' ice-battered waste,
To drop my anchor in the Muses' port,
And have my frail bark in strong iron cased,
That soon must be by fiercest tempest chased,
Fronting all winter's utmost rage severe :
Now, while short days the year's conclusion haste,
I'll stop at home with festive Christmas dear,
Singing my tale thus far the fireside group to cheer.

END OF CANTO I.

A

SONG OF CHRISTMAS.

A SONG OF CHRISTMAS.

———✦———

I

WHAT solemn strain—
Floats thro' the dark ? or dreams the brain ?
    What gentlest minstrels make
Soft music and the seal of slumber break ?
    It is 'the Waits'—they bring
Old Christmas back, and his glad welcome sing ;
    Who knows not that blithe band
With matin carol waking wintry land ?
    I knew them well of yore,
Where my sweet Sarum's natal spire doth soar,—
    Under night's muffling hood,
Hard by the elms glad morn's approach they wooed ;—
    From balmy sleep's snug nest
I heard, and joy and wonder filled my breast.
    May none such heralds scorn,
Whose cheerful notes usher the Christmas dawn ;
    Of sun, of earth, of sea,
He'd tire, of Christmas who could tirèd be :—
    Oh ! dull and desert heart,
That lov'st not Christmas, far from me depart :—
    But hark ! I hear the bells—
Far, near, loud, low, wild, wild their hubbub swolls,—
    Away I'll fly, and join the rout
Crowding the joyous street, and shout with them that
    shout.

II

Hark! how the bells with their merry merry chime,
      Spontaneous of rhyme,
Backwards, forwards swinging, louder, lower ringing
      In harmonious time,
With a clatter and a crash, and a silver dash and clash
      To the glad glad birth
      Of Christmas 'pon the earth,
Welcome, welcome, welcome seem to be singing—
      To the glad birth
      Of Christmas mirth,
Welcome, welcome, welcome, triply ringing !

      O'er moor, o'er fell,
      Up hill, down dell,
From tower to tower with one desire
      Bell answers bell,
      Spire nods to spire,
Country to town, to country town doth tell,—
      ' The foe of pain
      ' Is here again,
' Our new old friend, in spotless white attire,
      ' Christmas is here,
      ' Glad news, good cheer,
' Crown the full festive board, and feed the flaming fire.'

Welcome in cottage, welcome in hall,
Welcome in country, welcome in town,
      Market and street
      Where all folk meet,
To the rich and the poor, the great and the small,
To the lowest that lives by sweat of his brow,
To the lady that wears the sceptre and crown ;

Both old and young
Thee welcome now,
Whose laugh hides no malice, nor smile turns to frown;
True welcome, blithe welcome, gay welcome be rung;
Thou art old, thou art cold,—
But thy blue veins within still the warm blood is rolled.

III

Old man with silver beard and hair of snow,
Steps tott'ring as they go,—
Still shines thy mirthsome eye, thou'rt youthful yet,
And well therefore is set
The holly on thy head with glossy sheen
Of liveliest evergreen,
Where in and out, like tiny lamp ablaze,
The coy red berry strays;
And well with thee that hopping bird doth come
For whom all fling the crumb,
Robin, our homely pet with scarlet breast,
The open'd window's guest,
Who, when all pipers else forsake the year,
Warbles so sweet and clear,
That cross dull Winter stooping asks, 'What's this
'So small chirps not amiss?'

Hark! once more, the bells!
How their joyaunce swells!
O'er hill and dale again and far extending plain;
'For he is come,' they cry,
'For he is come with fife and drum,
'With band and song and dance,

' With glee and melody,
' And jolly countenance,
' The wine-cup come to quaff
' With loud uproarious laugh,
' For a boist'rous man is he, like the hurly-burly sea,—
' Yet comes he meek and mild
' Like sweetly smiling child,
' For a tender soul has he, kind as lamb upon the lea.'
Oh! ring the bells, ring low!
Oh! ring the bells, ring wild,
While he tramples down the snow
With his glory of laughter, deep tears lie below,
A mighty manly heart, but simple as a child.

IV

With good cheer and open brow
Wont to come, come Christmas now,
Bringing ease for old and weary,
Balm for broken heart and dreary,
Help and comfort for the poor,
Something sweet for ev'ry door,
Thou of blessings hast galore ;—
For the hungry findest food,
Hope for sad desponding mood,
For poor souls that houseless roam
Ready roof and hearty home ;—
For the shiv'rer clothes and fire.
All things bad from thee retire :
Evil passions of the mind,
Misanthrope who hates his kind,
Griping Avarice, thorny Care,
Vanity that loves a stare,
Selfish Pride, who hugs his chain,
Malice glorying in pain,

All fly thee ;—but Joy and Glee
Follow and warm Charity
Thy most blest society,
Seeking ever with delight
Household faces to unite ;—
Thou, an universal father,
All around the hearth dost gather,
Where if haply some sad eye
Light on chair of vacancy,
Mirth-eclipsing shadow creeps
And awhile heart inly weeps
For one deep-laid in churchyard green
Low in grave, no longer seen,
Where dark cypress, darker yew
Make black night of blackest hue ;—
Or the gentle mind meanders
O'er wide trackless sands where wanders
Some advent'rous soul best loved,
All by dangers dread unmoved,
Tracking wilderness of waste,
Or tumbled prone in voiceless haste
From fierce simoom's volcanic breath,
Winged with horror, winged with death.
But the grey sire's fancy follows
Where away on lonely billows
Some blithe curly-headed boy,
His old bosom's fondest joy,
Up and down the world doth roam,
Soused by salt sea's flying foam,—
Or ice-beset, who knows, afar
Under beam of moon and star
In empty land of sleep and night,
Where Dan Sol stints half his light,
On the dim outskirts of the world,
Where old Chaos blind has hurled

The piled icebergs' spectral host,
Warders weird of loveless coast,
That in glimmering twilight glare
Like Polypheme with eyeless stare,
When the giants' rabble rout
Asked him of his orb put out ;—
There the white bears prowl and pry
For the dozing seals that lie,
There 'neath wintry dome of snow
Innuits keep their lamp aglow,
There in windy tempest's van
Swift Aurora spreads her fan,
Thro' whose thin transparent screen
May the dimpling stars be seen
As at hide-and-seek to play,
All bewildered of their way ;—
There alone, the ship their hut,
Far apart with Nature shut,
My brave tars who sailed away
In the merry month of May,
Bid adieu to carking care
Keeping Christmas bill of fare,
And of absent friends oft think
Who to them health gaily drink,
Health, and hope, and sweet success,
And best prayer ' May God them bless.'
Homewards, homewards now I'm turning,
Happy spectacle discerning,
Where around the blazing hearth
Circles universal mirth ;
Riddle, jest, and joke abound ;
Frequent louder laughs resound,
When to query framed with care
Crooked answer's dull despair

Hobbles round the merry party,
Peal on peal re-echoing hearty.
Next the youngsters quake to hear
Ancient grandam's tale of fear,
Then up, when quiet sports are done,
Suits wild noise and madcap fun,
Flying far with swift alarms
From groping blind-man's outspread arms,
Who feeling for them out of sight,
Panic makes and whispered fright.
These snatch with half-reluctant soul
Brandied plum from lurid bowl,
Those attracts to magic game,
Twilight dusk of covert flame,
As to and fro athwart the sheet
Mimic shadows follow fleet.
But hark! what splendid din ascending,
What shouts of joy the rafters rending
Tell of the tree that starts to light
Flashing on the dazzled sight,
Thousand treasures there I ween,
Hanging bough and leaf between.
See—the Mummers now are met
In the hall with parts well set;
There the cruel Turkish knight
Kills the rest in fearful fight,
Till brave St. George to rescue hastes
And swift to ground vile Paynim casts,
Then away to play elsewhere
In pink and white so debonair.
Lo! Night half her journey measures,
Straight away to other pleasures,
Better betters still what's best,
Ever last outdoes the rest;

Now songs and glees and games are over,
Strikes up the band, the floors uncover,
Ev'ry little lord and lady
For the ball stands spruce and ready,
See commence the mazy dance,
Now to retreat, now to advance,
Now separate, now intertwined,
In labyrinth or alone they wind,—
A linkèd chain thread in and out,
Or coupled whirl the room about,
Till if chance their footsteps carry
Where the glist'ning bough doth tarry,
Whose white berries gem the spray,
Like to moisten'd pearls' dim ray,
Forfeit sweet must neither miss,
Gentle forfeit of a kiss.
But see in heaven's lamplit arc,
Thro' the broad bosom of the dark,
Star 'pon star in rapid race
From the welkin drops apace,
And the round world rolls once more
Towards the great sun's eastern door.
Ne'er Night knew such merry madness,
Nor felt so loth to quit such gladness,
As 'neath arch of hands all bend
Sequent pairs, and sports have end,
Then off to poppy Morpheus creep,
Low lulled in lap of silver sleep.

v

So speeds once more away
  The festive time,
With mirth, and dance, and holly spray,—
  So ends my rhyme.

So farewell Christmas—but if such delights
Thou canst beget, such happy harmless nights,
  We'll ever welcome thee with song,
  And the glad night prolong,—
Culling fresh gloss of greenest holly
  With red ripe berry shining,—
So well thy wisdom teaches to shun folly,
  To seasonable joys our hearts inclining,
And innocentest fun the cure of melancholy.

LONDON
PRINTED BY SPOTTISWOODE AND CO.
NEW-STREET SQUARE

GENERAL LIST OF WORKS

PUBLISHED BY

MESSRS. LONGMAN, GREEN, AND CO.

PATERNOSTER ROW, LONDON.

———❦———

Historical Works.

The **HISTORY of ENGLAND** from the Fall of Wolsey to the Death of Elizabeth. By JAMES ANTHONY FROUDE, M.A. late Fellow of Exeter College, Oxford. Third Edition of the First Eight Volumes.

VOLS. I to IV. the Reign of Henry VIII. Third Edition, 54s.

VOLS. V. and VI. the Reigns of Edward VI. and Mary. Third Edition, 28s.

VOLS. VII. and VIII. the Reign of Elizabeth, VOLS. I. and II. Third Edition, 28s.

The **HISTORY of ENGLAND** from the Accession of James II. By Lord MACAULAY. Three Editions as follows.

LIBRARY EDITION, 5 vols. 8vo. £4.

CABINET EDITION, 8 vols. post 8vo. 48s.

PEOPLE'S EDITION, 4 vols. crown 8vo. 16s.

REVOLUTIONS in ENGLISH HISTORY. By ROBERT VAUGHAN, D.D. 3 vols. 8vo. 45s.

VOL. I. Revolutions of Race, 15s.

VOL. II. Revolutions in Religion, 15s.

VOL. III. Revolutions in Government, 15s.

The **HISTORY of ENGLAND** during the Reign of George the Third. By WILLIAM MASSEY, M.P. 4 vols. 8vo. 48s.

The **CONSTITUTIONAL HISTORY of ENGLAND**, since the Accession of George III. 1760—1860. By THOMAS ERSKINE MAY, C.B. 2 vols. 8vo. 33s.

LIVES of the QUEENS of ENGLAND, from State Papers and other Documentary Sources: comprising a Domestic History of England from the Conquest to the Death of Queen Anne. By AGNES STRICKLAND. Revised Edition, with many Portraits. 8 vols. post 8vo. 60s.

A

LECTURES on the HISTORY of ENGLAND. By WILLIAM LONG-
MAN. VOL. I. from the earliest times to the Death of King Edward II. with
6 Maps, a coloured Plate, and 53 Woodcuts. 8vo. 15s.

A CHRONICLE of ENGLAND, from B.C. 55 to A.D. 1485 ; written
and illustrated by J. E. DOYLE. With 81 Designs engraved on Wood and
printed in Colours by E. Evans. 4to. 42s.

HISTORY of CIVILISATION. By HENRY THOMAS BUCKLE. 2 vols.
Price £1 17s.

   VOL. I. *England and France*, Fourth Edition, 21s.

   VOL. II. *Spain and Scotland*, Second Edition, 16s.

DEMOCRACY in AMERICA. By ALEXIS DE TOCQUEVILLE. Translated by HENRY REEVE, with an Introductory Notice by the Translator.
2 vols. 8vo. 21s.

The SPANISH CONQUEST in AMERICA, and its Relation to the
History of Slavery and to the Government of Colonies. By ARTHUR HELPS.
4 vols. 8vo. £3. VOLS. I. and II. 28s. VOLS. III. and IV. 16s. each.

HISTORY of the REFORMATION in EUROPE in the Time of
Calvin. By J. H. MERLE D'AUBIGNE, D.D. VOLS. I. and II. 8vo. 28s. and
VOL. III. 12s.

LIBRARY HISTORY of FRANCE, in 5 vols. 8vo. By EYRE EVANS
CROWE. VOL. I. 14s. VOL. II. 15s. VOL. III. 16s. VOL. IV. nearly ready.

LECTURES on the HISTORY of FRANCE. By the late Sir JAMES
STEPHEN, LL.D. 2 vols. 8vo. 24s.

The HISTORY of GREECE. By C. THIRLWALL, D.D., Lord Bishop
of St. David's. 8 vols. 8vo. £3; or in 8 vols. fcp. 28s.

The TALE of the GREAT PERSIAN WAR, from the Histories of
Herodotus. By the Rev. G. W. COX, M.A. late Scholar of Trin. Coll. Oxon.
Fcp. 8vo. 7s. 6d.

ANCIENT HISTORY of EGYPT, ASSYRIA, and BABYLONIA. By
the Author of 'Amy Herbert.' Fcp. 8vo. 6s.

CRITICAL HISTORY of the LANGUAGE and LITERATURE of
Ancient Greece. By WILLIAM MURE, of Caldwell. 5 vols. 8vo. £3 9s.

HISTORY of the LITERATURE of ANCIENT GREECE. By Professor K. O. MÜLLER. Translated by the Right Hon. Sir GEORGE CORNE-
WALL LEWIS, Bart. and by J. W. DONALDSON, D.D. 3 vols. 8vo. 36s.

HISTORY of the ROMANS under the EMPIRE. By the Rev.
CHARLES MERIVALE, B.D. 7 vols. 8vo. with Maps, £5.

The FALL of the ROMAN REPUBLIC: a Short History of the Last
Century of the Commonwealth. By the Rev. CHARLES MERIVALE, B.D.
12mo. 7s. 6d.

The BIOGRAPHICAL HISTORY of PHILOSOPHY, from its Origin
in Greece to the Present Day. By GEORGE HENRY LEWES. Revised and
enlarged Edition. 8vo. 16s.

HISTORY of the INDUCTIVE SCIENCES. By WILLIAM WHEWELL,
D.D. F.R.S. Master of Trin. Coll. Cantab. Third Edition. 3 vols. crown
8vo. 24s.

CRITICAL and HISTORICAL ESSAYS contributed to the *Edinburgh Review*. By the Right Hon. LORD MACAULAY.

LIBRARY EDITION, 3 vols. 8vo. 36s.

TRAVELLER'S EDITION, in 1 vol. 21s.

In POCKET VOLUMES, 3 vols. fcp. 21s.

PEOPLE'S EDITION, 2 vols. crown 8vo. 8s.

EGYPT'S PLACE in UNIVERSAL HISTORY; an Historical Investigation. By C. C. J. BUNSEN, D.D. Translated by C. H. COTTRELL, M.A. With many Illustrations. 4 vols. 8vo. £5 8s. VOL. V. is nearly ready.

MAUNDER'S HISTORICAL TREASURY; comprising a General Introductory Outline of Universal History, and a series of Separate Histories. Fcp. 8vo. 10s.

HISTORICAL and CHRONOLOGICAL ENCYCLOPÆDIA, presenting in a brief and convenient form Chronological Notices of all the Great Events of Universal History. By B. B. WOODWARD, F.S.A. Librarian to the Queen.
[*In the press.*

HISTORY of CHRISTIAN MISSIONS; their Agents and their Results By T. W. M. MARSHALL. 2 vols. 8vo. 24s.

HISTORY of the EARLY CHURCH, from the First Preaching of the Gospel to the Council of Nicæa, A.D. 325. By the Author of 'Amy Herbert.' Fcp. 8vo. 4s. 6d.

HISTORY of WESLEYAN METHODISM. By GEORGE SMITH, F.A.S. New Edition, with Portraits, in 31 parts. Price 6d. each.

HISTORY of MODERN MUSIC; a Course of Lectures delivered at the Royal Institution. By JOHN HULLAH, Professor of Vocal Music in King's College and in Queen's College, London. Post 8vo. 8s. 6d.

HISTORY of MEDICINE, from the Earliest Ages to the Present Time. By EDWARD MERYON, M.D. F.G.S. Vol. I. 8vo. 12s. 6d.

Biography and Memoirs.

SIR JOHN ELIOT, a Biography: 1590—1632. By JOHN FORSTER. With Two Portraits on Steel from the Originals at Port Eliot. 2 vols. crown 8vo. 30s.

LETTERS and LIFE of FRANCIS BACON, including all his Occasional Works. Collected and edited, with a Commentary, by J. SPEDDING, Trin. Coll. Cantab. VOLS. I. and II. 8vo. 24s.

LIFE of ROBERT STEPHENSON, F.R.S. By J. C. JEAFFRESON, Barrister-at-Law; and WILLIAM POLE, F.R.S. Memb. Inst. Civ. Eng. With 2 Portraits and many Illustrations. 2 vols. 8vo. [*Nearly ready.*

APOLOGIA pro VITA SUA: being a Reply to a Pamphlet entitled 'What then does Dr. Newman mean?' By JOHN HENRY NEWMAN, D.D. 8vo. 14s.

LIFE of the DUKE of WELLINGTON. By the Rev. G. R. GLEIG, M.A. Popular Edition, carefully revised; with copious Additions. Crown 8vo. 5s.

Brialmont and Gleig's Life of the Duke of Wellington. 4 vols. 8vo. with Illustrations, £2 14s.

Life of the Duke of Wellington, partly from the French of M. BRIALMONT, partly from Original Documents. By the Rev. G. R. GLEIG, M.A. 8vo. with Portrait, 15s.

FATHER MATHEW: a Biography. By JOHN FRANCIS MAGUIRE, M.P. Second Edition, with Portrait. Post 8vo. 12s. 6d.

Rome; its Ruler and its Institutions. By the same Author. New Edition in preparation.

LIFE of AMELIA WILHELMINA SIEVEKING, from the German. Edited, with the Author's sanction, by CATHERINE WINKWORTH. Post 8vo. with Portrait, 12s.

FELIX MENDELSSOHN'S LETTERS from *Italy and Switzerland,* translated by LADY WALLACE. Third Edition, with Notice of MENDELSSOHN'S Life and Works, by Henry F. CHORLEY; and *Letters from 1833 to 1847,* translated by Lady WALLACE. New Edition, with Portrait. 2 vols. crown 8vo. 5s. each.

DIARIES of a LADY of QUALITY, from 1797 to 1844. Edited, with Notes, by A. Hayward, Q.C. Second Edition. Post 8vo. 10s. 6d.

RECOLLECTIONS of the late WILLIAM WILBERFORCE, M.P. for the County of York during nearly 30 Years. By J. S. HARFORD, D.C.L. F.R.S. Post 8vo. 7s.

LIFE and CORRESPONDENCE of THEODORE PARKER. By JOHN WEISS. With 2 Portraits and 19 Wood Engravings. 2 vols. 8vo. 30s.

SOUTHEY'S LIFE of WESLEY. Fifth Edition. Edited by the Rev. C. C. SOUTHEY, M.A. Crown 8vo. 7s. 6d.

THOMAS MOORE'S MEMOIRS, JOURNAL, and CORRESPONDENCE. Edited and abridged from the First Edition by Earl RUSSELL. Square crown 8vo. with 8 Portraits, 12s. 6d.

MEMOIR of the Rev. SYDNEY SMITH. By his Daughter, Lady HOLLAND. With a Selection from his Letters, edited by Mrs. AUSTIN. 2 vols. 8vo. 28s.

LIFE of WILLIAM WARBURTON, D.D. Bishop of Gloucester from 1760 to 1779. By the Rev. J. S. WATSON, M.A. 8vo. with Portrait, 18s.

FASTI EBORACENSES: Lives of the Archbishops of York. By the late Rev. W. H. DIXON, M.A. Edited and enlarged by the Rev. J. RAINE, M.A. In 2 vols. Vol. I. comprising the lives to the Death of Edward III. 8vo. 15s.

VICISSITUDES of FAMILIES. By Sir BERNARD BURKE, Ulster King of Arms. FIRST, SECOND, and THIRD SERIES. 3 vols. crown 8vo. 12s. 6d. each.

BIOGRAPHICAL SKETCHES. By NASSAU W. SENIOR. Post 8vo.
price 10s. 6d.

ESSAYS in ECCLESIASTICAL BIOGRAPHY. By the Right Hon.
Sir J. STEPHEN, LL.D. Fourth Edition. 8vo. 14s.

ARAGO'S BIOGRAPHIES of DISTINGUISHED SCIENTIFIC MEN.
By FRANÇOIS ARAGO. Translated by Admiral W. H. SMYTH, F.R.S. the
Rev. B. POWELL, M.A. and R. GRANT, M.A. 8vo. 18s.

MAUNDER'S BIOGRAPHICAL TREASURY: Memoirs, Sketches, and
Brief Notices of above 12,000 Eminent Persons of All Ages and Nations.
Fcp. 8vo. 10s.

Criticism, Philosophy, Polity, &c.

PAPINIAN: a Dialogue on State Affairs between a Constitutional
Lawyer and a Country Gentleman about to enter Public Life. By GEORGE
ATKINSON, B.A. Oxon. Serjeant-at-Law. Post 8vo. 5s.

On REPRESENTATIVE GOVERNMENT. By JOHN STUART MILL.
Second Edition, 8vo. 9s.

Dissertations and Discussions. By the same Author. 2 vols. 8vo.
price 24s.

On Liberty. By the same Author. Third Edition. Post 8vo. 7s. 6d.

Principles of Political Economy. By the same. Fifth Edition.
2 vols. 8vo. 30s.

A System of Logic, Ratiocinative and Inductive. By the same.
Fifth Edition. Two vols. 8vo. 25s.

Utilitarianism. By the same. 8vo. 5s.

LORD BACON'S WORKS, collected and edited by R. L. ELLIS, M.A.
J. SPEDDING, M.A. and D. D. HEATH. Vols. L. to V. *Philosophical Works*
5 vols. 8vo. £4 6s. VOLS. VI. and VII. *Literary and Professional Works*
2 vols. £1 16s.

BACON'S ESSAYS with ANNOTATIONS. By R. WHATELY, D.D.
late Archbishop of Dublin. Sixth Edition. 8vo. 10s. 6d.

ELEMENTS of LOGIC. By R. WHATELY, D.D. late Archbishop of
Dublin. Ninth Edition. 8vo. 10s. 6d. crown 8vo. 4s. 6d.

Elements of Rhetoric. By the same Author. Seventh Edition.
8vo. 10s. 6d. crown 8vo. 4s. 6d.

English Synonymes. Edited by Archbishop WHATELY. 5th Edition.
Fcp. 8vo. 3s.

MISCELLANEOUS REMAINS from the Common-place Book of the
late Archbishop WHATELY. Edited by Miss E. J. WHATELY. Post 8vo. 6s.

ESSAYS on the **ADMINISTRATIONS** of **GREAT BRITAIN** from 1783 to 1830, contributed to the *Edinburgh Review* by the Right Hon. Sir G. C. LEWIS, Bart. Edited by the Right Hon. Sir E. HEAD, Bart. 8vo. with Portrait, 15s.

By the same Author.

A Dialogue on the Best Form of Government, 4s. 6d.

Essay on the Origin and Formation of the Romance Languages, price 7s. 6d.

Historical Survey of the Astronomy of the Ancients, 15s.

Inquiry into the Credibility of the Early Roman History, 2 vols. price 30s.

On the Methods of Observation and Reasoning in Politics, 2 vols. price 28s.

Irish Disturbances and Irish Church Question, 12s.

Remarks on the Use and Abuse of some Political Terms, 9s.

On Foreign Jurisdiction and Extradition of Criminals, 2s. 6d.

The Fables of Babrius, Greek Text with Latin Notes, PART I. 5s. 6d. PART II. 3s. 6d.

Suggestions for the Application of the Egyptological Method to Modern History, 1s.

An **OUTLINE** of the **NECESSARY LAWS** of **THOUGHT**: a Treatise on Pure and Applied Logic. By the Most Rev. W. THOMSON, D.D. Archbishop of York. Crown 8vo. 5s. 6d.

The **ELEMENTS** of **LOGIC**. By THOMAS SHEDDEN, M.A. of St. Peter's Coll. Cantab. Crown 8vo. [*Just ready.*]

ANALYSIS of Mr. **MILL'S SYSTEM** of **LOGIC**. By W. STEBBING, M.A. Fellow of Worcester College, Oxford. Post 8vo. [*Just ready.*]

SPEECHES of the **RIGHT HON. LORD MACAULAY**, corrected by Himself. 8vo. 12s.

LORD MACAULAY'S SPEECHES on **PARLIAMENTARY REFORM** in 1831 and 1832. 16mo. 1s.

A **DICTIONARY** of the **ENGLISH LANGUAGE**. By R. G. LATHAM, M.A. M.D. F.R.S. Founded on that of Dr. JOHNSON, as edited by the Rev. H. J. TODD, with numerous Emendations and Additions. Publishing in 36 Parts, price 3s. 6d. each, to form 2 vols. 4to.

The English Language. By the same Author. Fifth Edition. 8vo. price 18s.

Handbook of the English Language. By the same Author. Fourth Edition. Crown 8vo. 7s. 6d.

Elements of Comparative Philology. By the same Author. 8vo. 21s.

THESAURUS of ENGLISH WORDS and PHRASES, classified and arranged so as to facilitate the Expression of Ideas, and assist in Literary Composition. By P. M. ROGET, M. D. 14th Edition. Crown 8vo. 10s. 6d.

LECTURES on the SCIENCE of LANGUAGE, delivered at the Royal Institution. By MAX MULLER, M.A. Fellow of All Souls College, Oxford. FIRST SERIES, Fourth Edition. 8vo. 12s. SECOND SERIES, with 31 Woodcuts, price 18s.

The DEBATER; a Series of Complete Debates, Outlines of Debates, and Questions for Discussion. By F. ROWTON. Fcp. 8vo. 6s.

A COURSE of ENGLISH READING, adapted to every taste and capacity; or, How and What to Read. By the Rev. J. PYCROFT, B.A. Fcp. 8vo. 5s.

MANUAL of ENGLISH LITERATURE, Historical and Critical: with a Chapter on English Metres. By T. ARNOLD, B.A. Prof. of Eng. Lit. Cath. Univ. Ireland. Post 8vo. 10s. 6d.

SOUTHEY'S DOCTOR, complete in One Volume. Edited by the Rev. J. W. WARTER, B.D. Square crown 8vo. 12s. 6d.

HISTORICAL and CRITICAL COMMENTARY on the OLD TESTA-MENT; with a New Translation. By M. M. KALISCH, Ph.D. Vol. I. *Genesis*, 8vo. 18s. or adapted for the General Reader, 12s. VOL. II. *Exodus*, 15s. or adapted for the General Reader, 12s.

A Hebrew Grammar, with Exercises. By the same. PART I. *Outlines with Exercises*, 8vo. 12s. 6d. KEY, 5s. PART II. *Exceptional Forms and Constructions*, 12s. 6d.

A NEW LATIN-ENGLISH DICTIONARY. By the Rev. J. T. WHITE, M.A. of Corpus Christi College, and Rev. J. E. RIDDLE, M.A. of St. Edmund Hall, Oxford. Imperial 8vo. 42s.

A Diamond Latin-English Dictionary, or Guide to the Meaning, Quality, and Accentuation of Latin Classical Words. By the Rev. J. E. RIDDLE, M.A. 32mo. 4s.

A NEW ENGLISH-GREEK LEXICON, containing all the Greek Words used by Writers of good authority. By C. D. YONGE, B.A. Fourth Edition. 4to. 21s.

A LEXICON, ENGLISH and GREEK, abridged for the Use of Schools from his 'English-Greek Lexicon' by the Author, C. D. YONGE, B.A. Square 12mo. *[Just ready.*

A GREEK-ENGLISH LEXICON. Compiled by H. G. LIDDELL, D.D. Dean of Christ Church, and R. SCOTT, D.D. Master of Balliol. Fifth Edition. Crown 4to. 31s. 6d.

A Lexicon, Greek and English, abridged from LIDDELL and SCOTT'S *Greek-English Lexicon*. Tenth Edition. Square 12mo. 7s. 6d.

A PRACTICAL DICTIONARY of the FRENCH and ENGLISH LAN-GUAGES. By L. CONTANSEAU. 7th Edition. Post 8vo. 10s. 6d.

Contansean's Pocket Dictionary, French and English; being a close Abridgment of the above, by the same Author. 2nd Edition. 18mo. 5s.

NEW PRACTICAL DICTIONARY of the **GERMAN LANGUAGE**; German–English and English-German. By the Rev. W. L. BLACKLEY, M.A. and Dr. CARL MARTIN FRIEDLANDER. Post 8vo. [*In the press.*

Miscellaneous Works and Popular Metaphysics.

RECREATIONS of a **COUNTRY PARSON**: being a Selection of the Contributions of A. K. H. B. to *Fraser's Magazine*. SECOND SERIES. Crown 8vo. 3s. 6d.

The Common-place Philosopher in Town and Country. By the same Author. Crown 8vo. 3s. 6d.

Leisure Hours in Town; Essays Consolatory, Æsthetical, Moral, Social, and Domestic. By the same. Crown 8vo. 3s. 6d.

The Autumn Holidays of a Country Parson. By the same Author. 1 vol. [*Nearly ready.*

FRIENDS in COUNCIL: a Series of Readings and Discourses thereon. 2 vols. fcp. 8vo. 9s.

Friends in Council, SECOND SERIES. 2 vols. post 8vo. 14s.

Essays written in the Intervals of Business. Fcp. 8vo. 2s. 6d.

Companions of My Solitude. By the same Author. Fcp. 8vo. 3s. 6d.

LORD MACAULAY'S MISCELLANEOUS WRITINGS: comprising his Contributions to KNIGHT's *Quarterly Magazine*, Articles from the Edinburgh Review not included in his *Critical and Historical Essays*, Biographies from the *Encyclopædia Britannica*, Miscellaneous Poems and Inscriptions. 2 vols. 8vo. with Portrait, 21s.

The REV. SYDNEY SMITH'S MISCELLANEOUS WORKS; including his Contributions to the *Edinburgh Review*.

LIBRARY EDITION. 3 vols. 8vo. 36s.

TRAVELLER'S EDITION, in 1 vol. 21s.

In POCKET VOLUMES. 3 vols. 21s.

PEOPLE'S EDITION. 2 vols. crown 8vo. 8s.

Elementary Sketches of Moral Philosophy, delivered at the Royal Institution. By the same Author. Fcp. 8vo. 7s.

The Wit and Wisdom of Sydney Smith: a Selection of the most memorable Passages in his Writings and Conversation. 16mo. 7s. 6d.

From MATTER to SPIRIT: the Result of Ten Years' Experience in Spirit Manifestations. By C. D. with a preface by A. B. Post 8vo. 8s. 6d.

The HISTORY of the SUPERNATURAL in All Ages and Nations, and in all Churches, Christian and Pagan; Demonstrating a Universal Faith. By WILLIAM HOWITT. 2 vols. post 8vo. 18s.

CHAPTERS on MENTAL PHYSIOLOGY. By Sir HENRY HOLLAND, Bart. M.D. F.R.S. Second Edition. Post 8vo. 8s. 6d.

ESSAYS selected from **CONTRIBUTIONS** to the *Edinburgh Review.* By HENRY ROGERS. Second Edition. 3 vols. fcp. 21*s.*

The Eclipse of Faith ; or, a Visit to a Religious Sceptic. By the same Author. Tenth Edition. Fcp. 8vo. 5*s.*

Defence of the Eclipse of Faith, by its Author ; a rejoinder to Dr. Newman's *Reply.* Third Edition. Fcp. 8vo. 3*s.* 6*d.*

Selections from the Correspondence of R. E. H. Greyson. By the same Author. Third Edition. Crown 8vo. 7*s.* 6*d.*

Fulleriana, or the Wisdom and Wit of THOMAS FULLER, with Essay on his Life and Genius. By the same Author. 16mo. 2*s.* 6*d.*

Reason and Faith, reprinted from the *Edinburgh Review.* By the same Author. Fourth Edition. Fcp. 8vo. 1*s.* 6*d.*

An INTRODUCTION to MENTAL PHILOSOPHY, on the Inductive Method. By J. D. MORELL, M.A. LL.D. 8vo. 12*s.*

Elements of Psychology, containing the Analysis of the Intellectual Powers. By the same Author. Post 8vo. 7*s.* 6*d.*

The SENSES and the INTELLECT. By ALEXANDER BAIN, M.A. Professor of Logic in the University of Aberdeen. Second Edition. 8vo. price 15*s.*

The Emotions and the Will, by the same Author ; completing a Systematic Exposition of the Human Mind. 8vo. 15*s.*

On the Study of Character, including an Estimate of Phrenology. By the same Author. 8vo. 9*s.*

HOURS WITH THE MYSTICS: a Contribution to the History of Religious Opinion. By ROBERT ALFRED VAUGHAN, B.A. Second Edition. 2 vols. crown 8vo. 12*s.*

PSYCHOLOGICAL INQUIRIES, or Essays intended to illustrate the Influence of the Physical Organisation on the Mental Faculties. By Sir B. C. BRODIE, Bart. Fcp. 8vo. 5*s.* PART II. Essays intended to illustrate some Points in the Physical and Moral History of Man. Fcp. 8vo. 5*s.*

The PHILOSOPHY of NECESSITY ; or Natural Law as applicable to Mental, Moral, and Social Science. By CHARLES BRAY. Second Edition. 8vo. 9*s.*

The Education of the Feelings and Affections. By the same Author. Third Edition. 8vo. 3*s.* 6*d.*

CHRISTIANITY and COMMON SENSE. By Sir WILLOUGHBY JONES, Bart. M.A. Trin. Coll. Cantab. 8vo. 6*s.*

Astronomy, Meteorology, Popular Geography, &c.

OUTLINES of ASTRONOMY. By Sir J. F. W. HERSCHEL, Bart. M.A. Seventh Edition, revised ; with Plates and Woodcuts. 8vo. 18*s.*

ARAGO'S POPULAR ASTRONOMY. Translated by Admiral W. H. Smyth, F.R.S. and R. Grant, M.A. With 25 Plates and 358 Woodcuts. 2 vols. 8vo. £2 5s.

Arago's Meteorological Essays, with Introduction by Baron Humboldt. Translated under the superintendence of Major-General E. Sabine, R.A. 8vo. 18s.

The **WEATHER-BOOK;** a Manual of Practical Meteorology. By Rear-Admiral Robert Fitz Roy, R.N. F.R.S. Third Edition, with 16 Diagrams. 8vo. 15s.

SAXBY'S WEATHER SYSTEM, or Lunar Influence on Weather, By S. M. Saxby, R.N. Principal Instructor of Naval Engineers, H.M. Steam Reserve. Second Edition. Post 8vo. 4s.

DOVE'S LAW of STORMS considered in connexion with the ordinary Movements of the Atmosphere. Translated by R. H. Scott, M.A. T.C.D. 8vo. 10s. 6d.

CELESTIAL OBJECTS for COMMON TELESCOPES. By the Rev. T. W. Webb, M.A. F.R.A.S. With Map of the Moon, and Woodcuts. 16mo. 7s.

PHYSICAL GEOGRAPHY for SCHOOLS and GENERAL READERS. By M. F. Maury, LL.D. Author of 'Physical Geography of the Sea,' &c. Fcp. 8vo. with 2 Plates, 2s. 6d.

A DICTIONARY, Geographical, Statistical, and Historical, of the various Countries, Places, and Principal Natural Objects in the World. By J. R. M'Culloch, Esq. With 6 Maps. 2 vols. 8vo. 63s.

A GENERAL DICTIONARY of GEOGRAPHY, Descriptive, Physical, Statistical, and Historical: forming a complete Gazetteer of the World. By A. Keith Johnston, F.R.S.E. 8vo. 30s.

A MANUAL of GEOGRAPHY, Physical, Industrial, and Political. By W. Hughes, F.R.G.S. Professor of Geography in King's College, and in Queen's College, London. With 6 Maps. Fcp. 8vo. 7s. 6d.

Or in Two Parts:—Part I. Europe, 3s. 6d. Part II. Asia, Africa, America, Australasia, and Polynesia, 4s.

The **Geography of British History;** a Geographical description of the British Islands at Successive Periods, from the Earliest Times to the Present Day. By the same. With 6 Maps. Fcp. 8vo. 8s. 6d.

The **BRITISH EMPIRE;** a Sketch of the Geography, Growth, Natural and Political Features of the United Kingdom, its Colonies and Dependencies. By Caroline Bray. With 5 Maps. Fcp. 8vo. 7s. 6d.

COLONISATION and COLONIES: a Series of Lectures delivered before the University of Oxford. By Herman Merivale, M.A. Professor of Political Economy. 8vo. 18s.

The **AFRICANS at HOME:** a popular Description of Africa and the Africans. By the Rev. R. M. Macbrair, M.A. Second Edition; including an Account of the Discovery of the Source of the Nile. With Map and 70 Woodcuts. Fcp. 8vo. 5s.

MAUNDER'S TREASURY of GEOGRAPHY, Physical, Historical, Descriptive, and Political. Completed by W. Hughes, F.R.G.S. With 7 Maps and 16 Plates. Fcp. 8vo. 10s.

Natural History and Popular Science.

The **ELEMENTS** of **PHYSICS** or **NATURAL PHILOSOPHY**. By NEIL ARNOTT, M.D. F.R.S. Physician Extraordinary to the Queen. Sixth Edition. PART I. 8vo. 10s. 6d.

HEAT CONSIDERED as a **MODE** of **MOTION**; a Course of Lectures delivered at the Royal Institution. By Professor JOHN TYNDALL, F.R.S. Crown 8vo. with Woodcuts, 12s. 6d.

VOLCANOS, the Character of their Phenomena, their Share in the Structure and Composition of the Surface of the Globe, &c. By G. POULETT SCROPE, M.P. F.R.S. Second Edition. 8vo. with illustrations, 15s.

A TREATISE on **ELECTRICITY**, in Theory and Practice. By A. DE LA RIVE, Prof. in the Academy of Geneva. Translated by C. V. WALKER, F.R.S. 3 vols. 8vo. with Woodcuts, £3 13s.

The **CORRELATION** of **PHYSICAL FORCES**. By W. R. GROVE, Q.C. V.P.R.S. Fourth Edition. 8vo. 7s. 6d.

The **GEOLOGICAL MAGAZINE**; or, Monthly Journal of Geology Edited by T. RUPERT JONES, F.G.S. Professor of Geology in the R. M. College, Sandhurst; assisted by J. C. WOODWARD, P.G.S. F.Z.S. British Museum. 8vo. with Illustrations, price 1s. 6d. monthly.

A GUIDE to **GEOLOGY**. By J. PHILLIPS, M.A. Professor of Geology in the University of Oxford. Fifth Edition; with Plates and Diagrams. Fcp. 8vo. 4s.

A GLOSSARY of **MINERALOGY**. By H. W. BRISTOW, F.G.S. of the Geological Survey of Great Britain. With 486 Figures. Crown 8vo. 12s.

PHILLIPS'S ELEMENTARY INTRODUCTION to **MINERALOGY**, with extensive Alterations and Additions, by H. J. BROOKE, F.R.S. and W. H. MILLER, F.G.S. Post 8vo. with Woodcuts, 18s.

VAN DER HOEVEN'S HANDBOOK of **ZOOLOGY**. Translated from the Second Dutch Edition by the Rev. W. CLARK, M.D. F.R.S. 2 vols. 8vo. with 24 Plates of Figures, 60s.

The **COMPARATIVE ANATOMY** and **PHYSIOLOGY** of the **VERTE**brate Animals. By RICHARD OWEN, F.R.S. D.C.L. 2 vols. 8vo. with upwards of 1,200 Woodcuts. [In the press.

HOMES WITHOUT HANDS: an Account of the Habitations constructed by various Animals, classed according to their Principles of Construction. By Rev. J. G. WOOD, M.A. F.L.S. Illustrations on Wood by G. Pearson, from Drawings by F. W. Keyl and E. A. Smith. In course of publication in 20 Parts, 1s. each.

MANUAL of **CŒLENTERATA**. By J. REAY GREENE, B.A. M.R.I.A. Edited by the Rev. J. A. GALBRAITH, M.A. and the Rev. S. HAUGHTON, M.D. Fcp. 8vo. with 39 Woodcuts. 5s.

Manual of Protozoa; with a General Introduction on the Principles of Zoology. By the same Author and Editors. Fcp. 8vo. with 16 Woodcuts, 2s.

Manual of the Metalloids. By J. APJOHN, M.D. F.R.S. and the same Editors. Fcp. 8vo. with 38 Woodcuts, 7s. 6d.

THE ALPS: Sketches of Life and Nature in the Mountains. By Baron H. Von Berlepsch. Translated by the Rev. L. Stephen, M.A. With 17 Illustrations. 8vo. 15s.

The SEA and its LIVING WONDERS. By Dr. G. Hartwig. Second (English) Edition. 8vo. with many Illustrations. 18s.

The TROPICAL WORLD. By the same Author. With 8 Chromo-xylographs and 172 Woodcuts. 8vo. 21s.

SKETCHES of the NATURAL HISTORY of CEYLON. By Sir J. Emerson Tennent, K.C.S. LL.D. With 82 Wood Engravings. Post 8vo. price 12s. 6d.

Ceylon. By the same Author. 5th Edition; with Maps, &c. and 90 Wood Engravings. 2 vols. 8vo. £2 10s.

MARVELS and MYSTERIES of INSTINCT; or, Curiosities of Animal Life. By G. Garratt. Third Edition. Fcp. 8vo. 7s.

HOME WALKS and HOLIDAY RAMBLES. By the Rev. C. A. Johns, B.A. F.L.S. Fcp. 8vo. with 10 Illustrations, 6s.

KIRBY and SPENCE'S INTRODUCTION to ENTOMOLOGY, or Elements of the Natural History of Insects. Seventh Edition. Crown 8vo. price 5s.

MAUNDER'S TREASURY of NATURAL HISTORY, or Popular Dictionary of Zoology. Revised and corrected by T. S. Cobbold, M.D. Fcp. 8vo. with 900 Woodcuts, 10s.

The TREASURY of BOTANY, on the Plan of Maunder's Treasury. By J. Lindley, M.D. and T. Moore, F.L.S. assisted by other Practical Botanists. With 16 Plates, and many Woodcuts from designs by W. H. Fitch. Fcp. 8vo. [In the press.

The ROSE AMATEUR'S GUIDE. By Thomas Rivers. 8th Edition. Fcp. 8vo. 4s.

The BRITISH FLORA; comprising the Phænogamous or Flowering Plants and the Ferns. By Sir W. J. Hooker, K.H. and G. A. Walker Arnott, LL.D. 12mo. with 12 Plates, 14s. or coloured, 21s.

BRYOLOGIA BRITANNICA; containing the Mosses of Great Britain and Ireland, arranged and described. By W. Wilson. 8vo. with 61 Plates 42s. or coloured, £4 4s.

The INDOOR GARDENER. By Miss Maling. Fcp. 8vo. with coloured Frontispiece, 5s.

LOUDON'S ENCYCLOPÆDIA of PLANTS; comprising the Specific Character, Description, Culture, History, &c. of all the Plants found in Great Britain. With upwards of 12,000 Woodcuts. 8vo. £3 13s. 6d.

Loudon's Encyclopædia of Trees and Shrubs; containing the Hardy Trees and Shrubs of Great Britain scientifically and popularly described. With 2,000 Woodcuts. 8vo. 50s.

HISTORY of the BRITISH FRESHWATER ALGÆ. By A. H. Hassall, M.D. With 100 Plates of Figures. 2 vols. 8vo. price £1 15s.

MAUNDER'S SCIENTIFIC and LITERARY TREASURY ; a Popular Encyclopædia of Science, Literature, and Art. Fcp. 8vo. 10s.

A DICTIONARY of SCIENCE, LITERATURE and ART ; comprising the History, Description, and Scientific Principles of every Branch of Human Knowledge. Edited by W. T. BRANDE, F.R.S.L. and E. Fourth Edition, revised and corrected. [*In the press.*

ESSAYS on SCIENTIFIC and other SUBJECTS, contributed to the *Edinburgh* and *Quarterly Reviews*. By Sir H. HOLLAND, Bart. M.D. Second Edition. 8vo. 14s.

ESSAYS from the EDINBURGH and QUARTERLY REVIEWS; with Addresses and other pieces. By Sir J. F. W. HERSCHEL, Bart, M.A. 8vo. 18s.

Chemistry, Medicine, Surgery, and the Allied Sciences.

A DICTIONARY of CHEMISTRY and the Allied Branches of other Sciences; founded on that of the late Dr. Ure. By HENRY WATTS, F.C.S. assisted by eminent Contributors. 4 vols. 8vo. in course of publication in Monthly Parts. VOL. I. 31s. 6d. and VOL. II. 26s. are now ready.

HANDBOOK of CHEMICAL ANALYSIS, adapted to the Unitary System of Notation: Based on Dr. H. Wills' *Anleitung zur chemischen Analyse*. By F. T. CONINGTON, M.A. F.C.S. Post 8vo. 7s. 6d.—TABLES of QUALITATIVE ANALYSIS to accompany the same, 2s. 6d.

A HANDBOOK of VOLUMETRICAL ANALYSIS. By ROBERT H. SCOTT, M.A. T.C.D. Post 8vo. 4s. 6d.

ELEMENTS of CHEMISTRY, Theoretical and Practical. By WILLIAM A. MILLER, M.D. LL.D. F.R.S. F.G.S. Professor of Chemistry, King's College, London. 3 vols. 8vo. £2 12s. PART I. CHEMICAL PHYSICS. Third Edition enlarged, 12s. PART II. INORGANIC CHEMISTRY. Second Edition, 20s. PART III. ORGANIC CHEMISTRY. Second Edition, 20s.

A MANUAL of CHEMISTRY, Descriptive and Theoretical. By WILLIAM ODLING, M.B. F.R.S. Lecturer on Chemistry at St. Bartholomew's Hospital. PART I. 8vo. 9s.

A Course of Practical Chemistry, for the use of Medical Students. By the same Author. PART I. crown 8vo. with Woodcuts, 4s. 6d. PART II. (completion) *just ready.*

The **DIAGNOSIS and TREATMENT of the DISEASES of WOMEN ;** including the Diagnosis of Pregnancy. By GRAILY HEWITT, M.D. Physician to the British Lying-in Hospital. 8vo. 16s.

LECTURES on the DISEASES of INFANCY and CHILDHOOD. By CHARLES WEST, M.D. &c. Fourth Edition, revised and enlarged. 8vo. 14s.

EXPOSITION of the SIGNS and SYMPTOMS of PREGNANCY ; with other Papers on subjects connected with Midwifery. By W. F. MONTGOMERY, M.A. M.D. M.R.I.A. 8vo. with Illustrations, 25s.

A SYSTEM of SURGERY, Theoretical and Practical. In Treatises by Various Authors, arranged and edited by T. HOLMES, M.A. Cantab. Assistant-Surgeon to St. George's Hospital. 4 vols. 8vo.

Vol. I.   General Pathology.   21s.

Vol. II.   Local Injuries—Diseases of the Eye.   21s.

Vol. III.   Operative Surgery.   Diseases of the Organs of Special Sense, Respiration, Circulation, Locomotion and Innervation. 21s.

Vol. IV. Diseases of the Alimentary Canal, of the Urino-genitary Organs, of the Thyroid, Mamma and Skin; with Appendix of Miscellaneous Subjects, and GENERAL INDEX.   [Early in October.

LECTURES on the PRINCIPLES and PRACTICE of PHYSIC. By THOMAS WATSON, M.D. Physician-Extraordinary to the Queen. Fourth Edition. 2 vols. 8vo. 34s.

LECTURES on SURGICAL PATHOLOGY. By J. PAGET. F.R.S. Surgeon-Extraordinary to the Queen. Edited by W. TURNER, M.B. 8vo. with 117 Woodcuts, 21s.

A TREATISE on the CONTINUED FEVERS of GREAT BRITAIN. By C. MURCHISON, M.D. Senior Physician to the London Fever Hospital. 8vo. with coloured Plates, 18s.

DEMONSTRATIONS of MICROSCOPIC ANATOMY; a Guide to the Examination of the Animal Tissues and Fluids in Health and Disease, for the use of the Medical and Veterinary Professions. Founded on a Course of Lectures delivered by Dr. HARLEY, Prof. in Univ. Coll. London. Edited by G. T. BROWN, late Vet. Prof. in the Royal Agric. Coll. Cirencester. 8vo. with Illustrations.   [Nearly ready.

ANATOMY, DESCRIPTIVE and SURGICAL. By HENRY GRAY, F.R.S. With 410 Wood Engravings from Dissections. Third Edition, by T. HOLMES, M.A. Cantab. Royal 8vo. 28s.

PHYSIOLOGICAL ANATOMY and PHYSIOLOGY of MAN. By the late R. B. TODD, M.D. F.R.S. and W. BOWMAN, F.R.S. of King's College. With numerous Illustrations. VOL. II. 8vo. 25s.

A New Edition of the FIRST VOLUME, by Dr. LIONEL S. BEALE, is preparing for publication.

The CYCLOPÆDIA of ANATOMY and PHYSIOLOGY. Edited by the late R. B. TODD, M.D. F.R.S. Assisted by nearly all the most eminent cultivators of Physiological Science of the present age. 5 vols. 8vo. with 2,853 Woodcuts, £6 6s.

A DICTIONARY of PRACTICAL MEDICINE. By J. COPLAND, M.D. F.R.S. Abridged from the larger work by the Author, assisted by J. C. COPLAND. 1 vol. 8vo.   [In the press.

Dr. Copland's Dictionary of Practical Medicine (the larger work). 3 vols. 8vo. £5 11s.

The WORKS of SIR B. C. BRODIE, Bart. Edited by CHARLES HAWKINS, F.R.C.S.E. 2 vols. 8vo.   [In the press.

MEDICAL NOTES and REFLECTIONS. By Sir H. HOLLAND, Bart. M.D. Third Edition. 8vo. 18s.

HOOPER'S MEDICAL DICTIONARY, or Encyclopædia of Medical Science. Ninth Edition, brought down to the present time, by ALEX. HENRY, M.D. 1 vol. 8vo. [In the press.

A MANUAL of MATERIA MEDICA and THERAPEUTICS, abridged from Dr. PEREIRA's Elements by F. J. FARRE, M.D. Cantab. assisted by R. BENTLEY, M.R.C.S. and by R. WARRINGTON, F.C.S. 1 vol. 8vo.

Dr. Pereira's Elements of Materia Medica and Therapeutics, Third Edition. By A. S. TAYLOR, M.D. and G. O. REES, M.D. 3 vols. 8vo. with numerous Woodcuts, £3 15s.

The Fine Arts, and Illustrated Editions.

The **NEW TESTAMENT of OUR LORD and SAVIOUR JESUS CHRIST.** Illustrated with numerous Engravings on Wood from the OLD MASTERS. Crown 4to. price 63s. cloth, gilt top; or price £3 5s. elegantly bound in morocco. [In October.

LYRA GERMANICA; Hymns for the Sundays and Chief Festivals of the Christian Year. Translated by CATHERINE WINKWORTH: 125 Illustrations on Wood drawn by J. LEIGHTON, F.S.A. Fcp. 4to. 21s.

CATS' and FARLIE'S MORAL EMBLEMS; with Aphorisms, Adages, and Proverbs of all Nations: comprising 121 Illustrations on Wood by J. LEIGHTON, F.S.A. with an appropriate Text by R. PIGOTT. Imperial 8vo. 31s. 6d.

BUNYAN'S PILGRIM'S PROGRESS: with 126 Illustrations on Steel and Wood by C. BENNETT; and a Preface by the Rev. C. KINGSLEY. Fcp. 4to. 21s.

The **HISTORY of OUR LORD,** as exemplified in Works of Art: with that of His Types, St. John the Baptist, and other Persons of the Old and New Testament. By Mrs. JAMESON and Lady EASTLAKE. Being the Fourth and concluding SERIES of 'Sacred and Legendary Art;' with 31 Etchings and 281 Woodcuts. 2 vols. square crown 8vo. 42s.

In the same Series, by Mrs. JAMESON.

Legends of the Saints and Martyrs. Fourth Edition, with 19 Etchings and 187 Woodcuts. 2 vols. 31s. 6d.

Legends of the Monastic Orders. Third Edition, with 11 Etchings and 88 Woodcuts. 1 vol. 21s.

Legends of the Madonna. Third Edition, with 27 Etchings and 165 Woodcuts. 1 vol. 21s.

Arts, Manufactures, &c.

ENCYCLOPÆDIA of ARCHITECTURE, Historical, Theoretical, and Practical. By JOSEPH GWILT. With more than 1,000 Woodcuts. 8vo. 42s.

TUSCAN SCULPTORS, their Lives, Works, and Times. With Illustrations from Original Drawings and Photographs. By CHARLES C. PERKINS. 2 vols. imperial 8vo.   [*In the press.*

The ENGINEER'S HANDBOOK; explaining the Principles which should guide the young Engineer in the Construction of Machinery. By C. S. LOWNDES. Post 8vo. 5s.

The ELEMENTS of MECHANISM, for Students of Applied Mechanics. By T. M. GOODEVE, M.A. Professor of Nat. Philos. in King's Coll. London. With 200 Woodcuts. Post 8vo. 6s. 6d.

URE'S DICTIONARY of ARTS, MANUFACTURES, and MINES. Re-written and enlarged by ROBERT HUNT, F.R.S. assisted by numerous gentlemen eminent in Science and the Arts. With 2,000 Woodcuts. 3 vols. 8vo. £4.

ENCYCLOPÆDIA of CIVIL ENGINEERING, Historical. Theoretical, and Practical. By E. CRESY, C.E. With above 3,000 Woodcuts. 8vo. 42s.

TREATISE on MILLS and MILLWORK. By W. FAIRBAIRN, C.E. F.R.S. With 18 Plates and 322 Woodcuts. 2 vols. 8vo. 32s. or each vol. separately, 16s.

Useful Information for Engineers. By the same Author. FIRST and SECOND SERIES, with many Plates and Woodcuts. 2 vols. crown 8vo. 21s. or each vol. separately, 10s. 6d.

The Application of Cast and Wrought Iron to Building Purposes. By the same Author. Third Edition, with Plates and Woodcuts.
[*Nearly ready.*

The PRACTICAL MECHANIC'S JOURNAL: An Illustrated Record of Mechanical and Engineering Science, and Epitome of Patent Inventions. 4to. price 1s. monthly.

The PRACTICAL DRAUGHTSMAN'S BOOK of INDUSTRIAL DESIGN. By W. JOHNSON, Assoc. Inst. C.E. With many hundred Illustrations. 4to. 28s. 6d.

The PATENTEE'S MANUAL; a Treatise on the Law and Practice of Letters Patent for the use of Patentees and Inventors. By J. and J. H. JOHNSON. Post 8vo. 7s. 6d.

The ARTISAN CLUB'S TREATISE on the STEAM ENGINE, in its various Applications to Mines, Mills, Steam Navigation, Railways and Agriculture. By J. BOURNE, C.E. Fifth Edition; with 37 Plates and 546 Woodcuts. 4to. 42s.

A Catechism of the Steam Engine, in its various Applications to Mines, Mills, Steam Navigation, Railways, and Agriculture. By the same Author. With 80 Woodcuts. Fcp. 8vo. 6s.

The STORY of the GUNS. By Sir J. EMERSON TENNENT, K.C.S. F.R.S. With 33 Woodcuts. Post 8vo. 7s. 6d.

The THEORY of WAR Illustrated by numerous Examples from History. By Lieut.-Col. P. L. MACDOUGALL. *Third Edition*, with 10 Plans. Post 8vo. 10s. 6d.

COLLIERIES and COLLIERS; A Handbook of the Law and leading. Cases relating thereto. By J. C. FOWLER, Barrister-at-Law. Fcp. 8vo. 6s.

The ART of PERFUMERY; the History and Theory of Odours, and the Methods of Extracting the Aromas of Plants. By Dr. PIESSE, F.C.S. Third Edition, with 53 Woodcuts. Crown 8vo. 10s. 6d.

Chemical, Natural, and Physical Magic, for Juveniles during the Holidays. By the same Author. With 30 Woodcuts. Fcp. 8vo. 3s. 6d.

The Laboratory of Chemical Wonders: a Scientific Mélange for Young People. By the same. Crown 8vo. 5s. 6d.

TALPA; or the Chronicles of a Clay Farm. By C. W. HOSKYNS, Esq. With 24 Woodcuts from Designs by G. CRUIKSHANK. 16mo. 5s. 6d.

H.R.H. the PRINCE CONSORT'S FARMS: An Agricultural Memoir. By JOHN CHALMERS MORTON. Dedicated by permission to Her Majesty the QUEEN. With 40 Wood Engravings. 4to. 52s. 6d.

Handbook of Farm Labour, Steam, Water, Wind, Horse Power, Hand Power, &c. By the same Author. 16mo. 1s. 6d.

Handbook of Dairy Husbandry; comprising the General Management of a Dairy Farm, &c. By the same. 16mo. 1s. 6d.

LOUDON'S ENCYCLOPÆDIA of AGRICULTURE: comprising the Laying-out, Improvement, and Management of Landed Property, and the Cultivation and Economy of the Productions of Agriculture. With 1,100 Woodcuts. 8vo. 31s. 6d.

London's Encylopædia of Gardening: Comprising the Theory and Practice of Horticulture, Floriculture, Arboriculture, and Landscape Gardening. With 1,000 Woodcuts. 8vo. 31s. 6d.

London's Encyclopædia of Cottage, Farm, and Villa Architecture and Furniture. With more than 2,000 Woodcuts. 8vo. 42s.

HISTORY of WINDSOR GREAT PARK and WINDSOR FOREST. By WILLIAM MENZIES, Resident Deputy Surveyor. Dedicated by permission to H. M. the QUEEN. With 2 Maps, and 20 Photographs by the EARL of CAITHNESS and Mr. BEMBRIDGE. Imperial folio, £8 8s.

BAYLDON'S ART of VALUING RENTS and TILLAGES, and Claims of Tenants upon Quitting Farms, both at Michaelmas and Lady-Day. Eighth Edition, adapted to the present time by J. C. MORTON.

Religious and Moral Works.

An EXPOSITION of the 39 ARTICLES, Historical and Doctrinal. By E. HAROLD BROWNE, D.D. Lord Bishop of Ely. Sixth Edition, 8vo. 16s.

The Pentateuch and the Elohistic Psalms, in reply to Bishop Colenso. By the same Author. 8vo. 2s.

Examination Questions on Bishop Browne's Exposition of the Articles. By the Rev. J. GORLE, M.A. Fcp. 3s. 6d.

FIVE LECTURES on the **CHARACTER** of **ST. PAUL**; being the Hulsean Lectures for 1862. By the Rev. J. S. HOWSON, D.D. Second Edition. 8vo. 9s.

A CRITICAL and **GRAMMATICAL COMMENTARY** on **ST. PAUL'S** Epistles. By C. J. ELLICOTT, D.D. Lord Bishop of Gloucester and Bristol. 8vo.

Galatians, Third Edition, 8s. 6d.

Ephesians, Third Edition, 8s. 6d.

Pastoral Epistles, Second Edition, 10s. 6d.

Philippians, Colossians, and Philemon, Second Edition, 10s. 6d.

Thessalonians, Second Edition, 7s. 6d.

Historical Lectures on the Life of our Lord Jesus Christ: being the Hulsean Lectures for 1859. By the same. Third Edition. 8vo. 10s. 6d.

The Destiny of the Creature; and other Sermons preached before the University of Cambridge. By the same. Post 8vo. 5s.

The Broad and the Narrow Way; Two Sermons preached before the University of Cambridge. By the same. Crown 8vo. 2s.

Rev. T. H. HORNE'S INTRODUCTION to the CRITICAL STUDY and Knowledge of the Holy Scriptures. Eleventh Edition, corrected and extended under careful Editorial revision. With 4 Maps and 22 Woodcuts and Facsimiles. 4 vols. 8vo. £3 13s. 6d.

Rev. T. H. Horne's Compendious Introduction to the Study of the Bible, being an Analysis of the larger work by the same Author. Re-edited by the Rev. JOHN AYRE, M.A. With Maps. &c. Post 8vo. 9s.

The TREASURY of BIBLE KNOWLEDGE, on the Plan of Maunder's Treasuries. By the Rev. JOHN AYRE, M.A. Fcp. 8vo. with Maps and Illustrations. [*In the press.*

The GREEK TESTAMENT; with Notes, Grammatical and Exegetical. By the Rev. W. WEBSTER, M.A. and the Rev. W. F. WILKINSON, M.A. 2 vols. 8vo. £2 4s.

    VOL. I. the Gospels and Acts, 20s.

    VOL. II. the Epistles and Apocalypse, 24s.

The FOUR EXPERIMENTS in Church and State; and the Conflicts of Churches. By Lord ROBERT MONTAGU, M.P. 8vo. 12s.

EVERY-DAY SCRIPTURE DIFFICULTIES explained and illustrated; Gospels of St. Matthew and St. Mark. By J. E. PRESCOTT, M.A. late Fellow of C. C. Coll. Cantab. 8vo. 9s.

The PENTATEUCH and BOOK of JOSHUA Critically Examined. By J. W. COLENSO, D.D. Lord Bishop of Natal. PART I. *the Pentateuch examined as an Historical Narrative.* 8vo. 6s. PART II. *the Age and Authorship of the Pentateuch Considered*, 7s. 6d. PART III. *the Book of Deuteronomy*, 8s. PART IV. *the First 11 Chapters of* Genesis *examined and separated, with Remarks on the Creation, the Fall, and the Deluge*, 10s. 6d.

The LIFE and EPISTLES of ST. PAUL. By W. J. CONYBEARE, M.A. late Fellow of Trin. Coll. Cantab. and J. S. HOWSON, D.D. Principal of the Collegiate Institution, Liverpool.

LIBRARY EDITION, with all the Original Illustrations, Maps, Landscapes on Steel, Woodcuts, &c. 2 vols. 4to. 48s.

INTERMEDIATE EDITION, with a Selection of Maps, Plates, and Woodcuts. 2 vols. square crown 8vo. 31s. 6d.

PEOPLE's EDITION, revised and condensed, with 46 Illustrations and Maps. 2 vols. crown 8vo. 12s.

The VOYAGE and SHIPWRECK of ST. PAUL; with Dissertations. on the Ships and Navigation of the Ancients. By JAMES SMITH, F.R.S. Crown 8vo. Charts, 8s. 6d.

HIPPOLYTUS and his AGE; or, the Beginnings and Prospects of Christianity. By Baron BUNSEN, D.D. 2 vols. 8vo. 30s.

Outlines of the Philosophy of Universal History, applied to Language and Religion: Containing an Account of the Alphabetical Conferences. By the same Author. 2 vols. 8vo. 33s.

Analecta Ante-Nicæna. By the same Author. 3 vols. 8vo. 42s.

THEOLOGIA GERMANICA. Translated by SUSANNAH WINKWORTH: with a Preface by the Rev. C. KINGSLEY; and a Letter by Baron BUNSEN. Fcp. 8vo. 5s.

INSTRUCTIONS in the DOCTRINE and PRACTICE of CHRIStianity, as an Introduction to Confirmation. By G. E. L. COTTON, D.D. Lord Bishop of Calcutta. 18mo. 2s. 6d.

ESSAYS on RELIGION and LITERATURE. By Cardinal WISEMAN, Dr. D. ROCK, F. H. LAING, and other Writers. Edited by H. E. MANNING, D.D. 8vo.

ESSAYS and REVIEWS. By the Rev. W. TEMPLE, D.D. the Rev. R. WILLIAMS, B.D. the Rev. B. POWELL, M.A. the Rev. H. B. WILSON, B.D. C. W. GOODWIN, M.A. the Rev. M. PATTISON, B.D. and the Rev. B. JOWETT, M.A. 11th Edition. Fcp. 8vo. 5s.

MOSHEIM'S ECCLESIASTICAL HISTORY. MURDOCK and SOAMES's Translation and Notes, re-edited by the Rev. W. STUBBS, M.A. 3 vols. 8vo. 45s.

The GENTILE and the JEW in the Courts of the Temple of Christ: an Introduction to the History of Christianity. From the German of Prof. DÖLLINGER, by the Rev. N. DARNELL, M.A. 2 vols. 8vo. 21s.

PHYSICO-PROPHETICAL ESSAYS, on the Locality of the Eternal Inheritance, its Nature and Character; the Resurrection Body; and the Mutual Recognition of Glorified Saints. By the Rev. W. LISTER, F.G.S. Crown 8vo. 6s.

BISHOP JEREMY TAYLOR'S ENTIRE WORKS: With Life by BISHOP HEBER. Revised and corrected by the Rev. C. P. EDEN, 10 vols. 8vo. £5 5s.

PASSING THOUGHTS on RELIGION. By the Author of ' Amy Herbert.' 8th Edition. Fcp. 8vo. 5s.

Thoughts for the Holy Week, for Young Persons. By the same Author. 2d Edition. Fcp. 8vo. 2s.

Night Lessons from Scripture. By the same Author. 2d Edition. 32mo. 3s.

Self-Examination before Confirmation. By the same Author. 32mo. price 1s. 6d.

Readings for a Month Preparatory to Confirmation, from Writers of the Early and English Church. By the same. Fcp. 4s.

Readings for Every Day in Lent, compiled from the Writings of Bishop JEREMY TAYLOR. By the same. Fcp. 8vo. 5s.

Preparation for the Holy Communion; the Devotions chiefly from the works of JEREMY TAYLOR. By the same. 32mo. 3s.

MORNING CLOUDS. Second Edition. Fcp. 8vo. 5s.

The Afternoon of Life. By the same Author. Second Edition. Fcp. 5s.

Problems in Human Nature. By the same. Post 8vo. 5s.

The WIFE'S MANUAL; or, Prayers, Thoughts, and Songs on Several Occasions of a Matron's Life. By the Rev. W. CALVERT, M.A. Crown 8vo. price 10s. 6d.

SPIRITUAL SONGS for the SUNDAYS and HOLIDAYS throughout the Year. By J. S. B. MONSELL, LL.D. Vicar of Egham. Third Edition. Fcp. 8vo. 4s. 6d.

HYMNOLOGIA CHRISTIANA: or, Psalms and Hymns selected and arranged in the order of the Christian Seasons. By B. H. KENNEDY, D.D. Prebendary of Lichfield. Crown 8vo. 7s. 6d.

LYRA SACRA; Hymns, Ancient and Modern, Odes and Fragments of Sacred Poetry. Edited by the Rev. B. W. SAVILE, M.A. Fcp. 8vo. 5s.

LYRA GERMANICA, translated from the German by Miss C. WINKWORTH. FIRST SERIES, Hymns for the Sundays and Chief Festivals; SECOND SERIES, the Christian Life. Fcp. 8vo. 5s. each SERIES.

Hymns from Lyra Germanica, 18mo. 1s.

LYRA EUCHARISTICA; Hymns and Verses on the Holy Communion, Ancient and Modern: with other Poems. Edited by the Rev. ORBY SHIPLEY, M.A. Second Edition, revised and enlarged. Fcp. 8vo. 7s. 6d.

Lyra Messianica; Hymns and Verses on the Life of Christ, Ancient and Modern; with other Poems. By the same Editor. Fcp. 8vo. 7s. 6d.

Lyra Mystica; Hymns and Verses on Sacred Subjects, Ancient and Modern. Forming a companion volume to the above, by the same Editor. Fcp. 8vo.   [Nearly ready.

LYRA DOMESTICA; Christian Songs for Domestic Edification. Translated from the *Psaltery and Harp* of C. J. P. SPITTA, and from other sources, by RICHARD MASSIE. FIRST and SECOND SERIES, fcp. 8vo. price 4s. 6d. each.

The CHORALE BOOK for ENGLAND; a complete Hymn-Book in accordance with the Services and Festivals of the Church of England: the Hymns translated by Miss C. WINKWORTH; the tunes arranged by Prof. W. S. BENNETT and OTTO GOLDSCHMIDT. Fcp. 4to. 10s. 6d.

Congregational Edition. Fcp. 8vo. price 1s. 6d.

Travels, Voyages, &c.

EASTERN EUROPE and WESTERN ASIA. Political and Social Sketches on Russia, Greece, and Syria. By HENRY A. TILLEY. With 6 Illustrations. Post 8vo. 10s. 6d.

EXPLORATIONS in SOUTH-WEST AFRICA, from Walvisch Bay to Lake Ngami and the Victoria Falls. By THOMAS BAINES. 8vo. with Map and Illustrations. [*In October.*

SOUTH AMERICAN SKETCHES; or, a Visit to Rio Janeiro, the Organ Mountains, La Plata, and the Paraná. By THOMAS W. HINCHLIFF, M.A. F.R.G.S. Post 8vo. with Illustrations, 12s. 6d.

EXPLORATIONS in LABRADOR. By HENRY Y. HIND, M.A. F.R.G.S. With Maps and Illustrations. 2 vols. 8vo. 32s.

The Canadian Red River and Assinniboine and Saskatchewan Exploring Expeditions. By the same Author. With Maps and Illustrations. 2 vols. 8vo. 42s.

The CAPITAL of the TYCOON; a Narrative of a Three Years' Residence in Japan. By Sir RUTHERFORD ALCOCK, K.C.B. 2 vols. 8vo. with numerous Illustrations, 42s.

LAST WINTER in ROME and other ITALIAN CITIES. By C. R. WELD, Author of 'The Pyrenees, West and East,' &c. 1 vol. post 8vo. with a Portrait of 'STELLA,' and Engravings on Wood from Sketches by the Author. [*In the Autumn.*

AUTUMN RAMBLES in NORTH AFRICA. By JOHN ORMSBY, of the Middle Temple, Author of the 'Ascent of the Grivola,' in 'Peaks, Passes, and Glaciers.' With 13 Illustrations on Wood from Sketches by the Author. Post 8vo. 8s. 6d.

PEAKS, PASSES, and GLACIERS; a Series of Excursions by Members of the Alpine Club. Edited by J. BALL, M.R.I.A. Fourth Edition; Maps, Illustrations, Woodcuts. Square crown 8vo. 21s.—TRAVELLERS' EDITION, condensed, 16mo. 5s. 6d.

Second Series, edited by E. S. KENNEDY, M.A. F.R.G.S. With many Maps and Illustrations. 2 vols. square crown 8vo. 42s.

Nineteen Maps of the Alpine Districts, from the First and Second Series of *Peaks, Passes, and Glaciers*. Price 7s. 6d.

The **DOLOMITE MOUNTAINS**. Excursions through Tyrol, Carinthia, Carniola, and Friuli in 1861, 1862, and 1863. By J. Gilbert and G. C. Churchill, F.R.G.S. With numerous Illustrations. Square crown 8vo. 21s.

MOUNTAINEERING in 1861; a Vacation Tour.   By Prof. J. Tyndall, F.R.S. Square crown 8vo. with 2 Views, 7s. 6d.

A **SUMMER TOUR** in the **GRISONS** and **ITALIAN VALLEYS** of the Bernina. By Mrs. Henry Freshfield. With 2 Coloured Maps and 4 Views. Post 8vo. 10s. 6d.

Alpine Byeways; or, Light Leaves gathered in 1859 and 1860.   By the same Authoress. Post 8vo. with Illustrations, 10s. 6d.

A **LADY'S TOUR ROUND MONTE ROSA**; including Visits to the Italian Valleys. With Map and Illustrations. Post 8vo. 14s.

GUIDE to the **PYRENEES**, for the use of Mountaineers.   By Charles Packe. With Maps, &c. and a new Appendix. Fcp. 6s.

GUIDE to the **CENTRAL ALPS**, including the Bernese Oberland, Eastern Switzerland, Lombardy, and Western Tyrol. By John Ball, M.R.I.A. Post 8vo. with 8 Maps, 7s. 6d. or with an Introduction on Alpine Travelling, and on the Geology of the Alps, 8s. 6d. The Introduction separately, 1s.

Guide to the Western Alps.   By the same Author.   With an Article on the Geology of the Alps by M. E. Desor. Post 8vo. with Maps, &c. 7s. 6d.

A **WEEK** at the **LAND'S END**. By J. T. Blight ; assisted by E. H. Rodd, R. Q. Couch, and J. Ralfs. With Map and 96 Woodcuts. Fcp. 8vo. 6s. 6d.

VISITS to **REMARKABLE PLACES**: Old Halls, Battle-Fields, and Scenes Illustrative of Striking Passages in English History and Poetry. By William Howitt. 2 vols. square crown 8vo. with Wood Engravings, price 25s.

The **RURAL LIFE** of **ENGLAND**.   By the same Author.   With Woodcuts by Bewick and Williams. Medium 8vo. 12s. 6d.

Works of Fiction.

LATE LAURELS: a Tale.   By the Author of 'Wheat and Tares.'   2 vols. post 8vo. 15s.

GRYLL GRANGE. By the Author of 'Headlong Hall.'   Post 8vo. price 7s. 6d.

A **FIRST FRIENDSHIP**.   [Reprinted from *Fraser's Magazine.*] Crown 8vo. 7s. 6d.

THALATTA ; or, the Great Commoner : a Political Romance.   Crown 8vo. 9s.

ATHERSTONE PRIORY. By L. N. COMYN. 2 vols. post 8vo. 21s.

Ellice: a Tale. By the same. Post 8vo. 9s. 6d.

The LAST of the OLD SQUIRES. By the Rev. J. W. WARTER, B.D. Second Edition. Fcp. 8vo. 4s. 6d.

TALES and STORIES by the Author of 'Amy Herbert,' uniform Edition, each Story or Tale in a single Volume.

AMY HERBERT, 2s. 6d.	IVORS, 3s. 6d.
GERTRUDE, 2s. 6d.	KATHARINE ASHTON, 3s. 6d.
EARL'S DAUGHTER, 2s. 6d.	MARGARET PERCIVAL, 5s.
EXPERIENCE OF LIFE, 2s. 6d.	LANETON PARSONAGE, 4s. 6d.
CLEVE HALL, 3s. 6d.	URSULA, 4s. 6d.

A Glimpse of the World. By the Author of 'Amy Herbert.' Fcp. 7s. 6d.

ESSAYS on FICTION; comprising Articles on Sir W. SCOTT, Sir E. B. LYTTON, Colonel SENIOR, Mr. THACKERAY, and Mrs. BEECHER STOWE. Reprinted chiefly from the *Edinburgh, Quarterly,* and *Westminster Reviews*; with large Additions. By NASSAU W. SENIOR. Post 8vo. 10s. 6d.

The GLADIATORS: A Tale of Rome and Judæa. By G. J. WHYTE MELVILLE. Crown 8vo.

Digby Grand, an Autobiography. By the same Author. 1 vol. 5s.

Kate Coventry, an Autobiography. By the same. 1 vol. 5s.

General Bounce, or the Lady and the Locusts. By the same. 1 vol. 5s.

Holmby House, a Tale of Old Northamptonshire. 1 vol. 5s.

Good for Nothing, or All Down Hill. By the same. 1 vol. 6s.

The Queen's Maries, a Romance of Holyrood. 1 vol. 6s.

The Interpreter, a Tale of the War. By the same. 1 vol. 5s.

TALES from GREEK MYTHOLOGY. By the Rev. G. W. COX, M.A. late Scholar of Trin. Coll. Oxon. Second Edition. Square 16mo. 3s. 6d.

Tales of the Gods and Heroes. By the same Author. Second Edition. Fcp. 8vo. 5s.

Tales of Thebes and Argos. By the same Author. Fcp. 8vo. 4s. 6d.

The WARDEN: a Novel. By ANTHONY TROLLOPE. Crown 8vo. 3s. 6d.

Barchester Towers: a Sequel to 'The Warden.' By the same Author. Crown 8vo. 5s.

The SIX SISTERS of the VALLEYS: an Historical Romance. By W. BRAMLEY-MOORE, M.A. Incumbent of Gerrard's Cross, Bucks. With 14 Illustrations on Wood. Crown 8vo. 5s.

Poetry and the Drama.

MOORE'S POETICAL WORKS, Cheapest Editions complete in 1 vol. including the Autobiographical Prefaces and Author's last Notes, which are still copyright. Crown 8vo. ruby type, with Portrait, 7s. 6d. or People's Edition, in larger type, 12s. 6d.

Moore's Poetical Works, as above, Library Edition, medium 8vo. with Portrait and Vignette, 21s. or in 10 vols. fcp. 3s. 6d. each.

TENNIEL'S EDITION of MOORE'S LALLA ROOKH, with 68 Wood Engravings from original Drawings and other Illustrations. Fcp. 4to. 21s.

Moore's Lalla Rookh. 32mo. Plate, 1s. 16mo. Vignette, 2s. 6d. Square crown 8vo. with 18 Plates, 15s.

MACLISE'S EDITION of MOORE'S IRISH MELODIES, with 161 Steel Plates from Original Drawings. Super-royal 8vo. 31s. 6d.

Moore's Irish Melodies, 32mo. Portrait, 1s. 16mo. Vignette, 2s. 6d. Square crown 8vo. with 18 Plates, 21s.

SOUTHEY'S POETICAL WORKS, with the Author's last Corrections and copyright Additions. Library Edition, in 1 vol. medium 8vo. with Portrait and Vignette, 14s. or in 10 vols. fcp. 3s. 6d. each.

LAYS of ANCIENT ROME; with *Ivry* and the *Armada*. By the Right Hon. LORD MACAULAY. 16mo. 4s. 6d.

Lord Macaulay's Lays of Ancient Rome. With 90 Illustrations on Wood, Original and from the Antique, from Drawings by G. SCHARF. Fcp. 4to. 21s.

POEMS. By JEAN INGELOW. Seventh Edition. Fcp. 8vo. 5s.

POETICAL WORKS of LETITIA ELIZABETH LANDON (L. E. L.) 2 vols. 16mo. 10s.

PLAYTIME with the POETS: a Selection of the best English Poetry for the use of Children. By a LADY. Crown 8vo. 5s.

The REVOLUTIONARY EPICK. By the Right Hon. BENJAMIN DISRAELI. Fcp. 8vo. 5s.

BOWDLER'S FAMILY SHAKSPEARE, cheaper Genuine Edition, complete in 1 vol. large type, with 36 Woodcut Illustrations, price 14s. or with the same ILLUSTRATIONS, in 6 pocket vols. 5s. each.

An ENGLISH TRAGEDY; Mary Stuart, from SCHILLER; and Mdlle. De Belle Isle, from A. DUMAS,—each a Play in 5 Acts, by FRANCES ANNE KEMBLE. Post 8vo. 12s.

Rural Sports, &c.

ENCYCLOPÆDIA of RURAL SPORTS; a complete Account, Historical, Practical, and Descriptive. of Hunting, Shooting, Fishing, Racing, &c. By D. P. BLAINE. With above 600 Woodcuts (20 from Designs by JOHN LEECH). 8vo. 42s.

COL. HAWKER'S INSTRUCTIONS to YOUNG SPORTSMEN in all that relates to Guns and Shooting. Revised by the Author's SON. Square crown 8vo. with Illustrations, 18s.

NOTES on RIFLE SHOOTING. By Captain HEATON, Adjutant of the Third Manchester Rifle Volunteer Corps. Fcp. 8vo. 2s. 6d.

The DEAD SHOT, or Sportsman's Complete Guide; a Treatise on the Use of the Gun, Dog-breaking, Pigeon-shooting, &c. By MARKSMAN. Fcp. 8vo. with Plates, 5s.

The CHASE of the WILD RED DEER in DEVON and SOMERSET. By C. P. COLLYNS. With Map and Illustrations. Square crown 8vo. 16s.

The FLY-FISHER'S ENTOMOLOGY. By ALFRED RONALDS. With coloured Representations of the Natural and Artificial Insect. 6th Edition; with 20 coloured Plates. 8vo. 14s.

HANDBOOK of ANGLING: Teaching Fly-fishing, Trolling, Bottom-fishing, Salmon-fishing; with the Natural History of River Fish, and the best modes of Catching them. By EPHEMERA. Fcp. Woodcuts, 5s.

The CRICKET FIELD; or, the History and the Science of the Game of Cricket. By J. PYCROFT, B.A. Trin. Coll. Oxon. 4th Edition. Fcp. 8vo. 5s.

The Cricket Tutor; a Treatise exclusively Practical. By the same. 16mo. 1s.

The HORSE'S FOOT, and HOW to KEEP IT SOUND. By W. MILES, Esq. 9th Edition, with Illustrations. Imp. 8vo. 12s. 6d.

A Plain Treatise on Horse-Shoeing. By the same Author. Post 8vo. with Illustrations, 2s.

General Remarks on Stables, and Examples of Stable Fittings. By the same. Imp. 8vo. with 13 Plates, 15s.

Remarks on Horses' Teeth, adapted to Purchasers. By the same Author. Crown 8vo. 1s. 6d.

The HORSE: with a Treatise on Draught. By WILLIAM YOUATT. New Edition, revised and enlarged. 8vo. with numerous Woodcuts, 10s. 6d.

The Dog. By the same Author. 8vo. with numerous Woodcuts, 6s.

The DOG in HEALTH and DISEASE. By STONEHENGE. With 70 Wood Engravings. Square crown 8vo. 15s.

The Greyhound. By the same. With many Illustrations. Square crown 8vo. 21s.

The OX; his Diseases and their Treatment: with an Essay on Parturition in the Cow. By J. R. DOBSON, M.R.C.V.S. Post 8vo. with Illustrations. *[Just ready.*

Commerce, Navigation, and Mercantile Affairs.

The **LAW** of **NATIONS** Considered as Independent Political Communities. By TRAVERS TWISS, D.C.L. Regius Professor of Civil Law in the University of Oxford. 2 vols. 8vo. 30s. or separately, PART I. *Peace*, 12s. PART II. *War*. 18s.

A **DICTIONARY**, Practical, Theoretical, and Historical, of Commerce and Commercial Navigation. By J. R. M'CULLOCH, Esq. 8vo. with Maps and Plans, 50s.

The **STUDY** of **STEAM** and the **MARINE ENGINE**, for Young Sea Officers. By S. M. SAXBY, R.N. Post 8vo. with 87 Diagrams, 5s. 6d.

A **NAUTICAL DICTIONARY**, defining the Technical Language relative to the Building and Equipment of Sailing Vessels and Steamers, &c. By ARTHUR YOUNG. Second Edition; with Plates and 150 Woodcuts. 8vo. 18s.

A **MANUAL** for **NAVAL CADETS**. By J. M'NEIL BOYD, late Captain R.N. Third Edition; with 240 Woodcuts and 11 coloured Plates. Post 8vo. 12s. 6d.

*** Every Cadet in the Royal Navy is required by the Regulations of the Admiralty to have a copy of this work on his entry into the Navy.

Works of Utility and General Information.

MODERN COOKERY for **PRIVATE FAMILIES**, reduced to a System of Easy Practice in a Series of carefully-tested Receipts. By ELIZA ACTON. Newly revised and enlarged; with 8 Plates, Figures, and 150 Woodcuts. Fcp. 8vo. 7s. 6d.

On **FOOD** and its **DIGESTION**; an Introduction to Dietetics. By W. BRINTON. M.D. Physician to St. Thomas's Hospital, &c. With 48 Woodcuts. Post 8vo. 12s.

ADULTERATIONS DETECTED; or Plain Instructions for the Discovery of Frauds in Food and Medicine. By A. H. HASSALL, M.D. Crown 8vo. with Woodcuts, 17s. 6d.

The **VINE** and its **FRUIT**, in relation to the Production of Wine. By JAMES L. DENMAN. Crown 8vo. 8s. 6d.

WINE, the **VINE**, and the **CELLAR**. By THOMAS G. SHAW. With 28 Illustrations on Wood. 8vo. 16s.

A **PRACTICAL TREATISE** on **BREWING**; with Formulæ for Public Brewers, and Instructions for Private Families. By W. BLACK. 8vo. 10s. 6d.

SHORT WHIST; its Rise, Progress, and Laws; with the Laws of Piquet, Cassino, Ecarté, Cribbage, and Backgammon. By Major A. Fcp. 8vo. 3s.

HINTS on **ETIQUETTE** and the **USAGES of SOCIETY**; with a Glance at Bad Habits. Revised, with Additions, by a LADY of RANK. Fcp. 8vo. 2s. 6d.

The CABINET LAWYER; a Popular Digest of the Laws of England, Civil and Criminal. 19th *Edition*, extended by the Author; including the Acts of the Sessions 1862 and 1883. Fcp. 8vo. 10s. 6d.

The PHILOSOPHY of HEALTH; or, an Exposition of the Physiological and Sanitary Conditions conducive to Human Longevity and Happiness. By SOUTHWOOD SMITH, M.D. Eleventh Edition, revised and enlarged: with New Plates, 8vo.   [Just ready.

HINTS to MOTHERS on the **MANAGEMENT** of their **HEALTH** during the Period of Pregnancy and in the Lying-in Room. By T. BULL, M.D. Fcp. 8vo. 5s.

The Maternal Management of Children in Health and Disease. By the same Author. Fcp. 8vo. 5s.

NOTES on HOSPITALS. By FLORENCE NIGHTINGALE. Third Edition, enlarged; with 13 Plans. Post 4to. 18s.

C. M. WILLICH'S POPULAR TABLES for ascertaining the Value of Lifehold, Leasehold, and Church Property, Renewal Fines, &c.; the Public Funds; Annual Average Price and Interest on Consols from 1731 to 1861; Chemical, Geographical, Astronomical, Trigonometrical Tables, &c. Post 8vo. 10s.

THOMSON'S TABLES of INTEREST, at Three, Four, Four and a Half, and Five per Cent. from One Pound to Ten Thousand and from 1 to 365 Days. 12mo. 3s. 6d.

MAUNDER'S TREASURY of KNOWLEDGE and LIBRARY of Reference: comprising an English Dictionary and Grammar, a Universal Gazetteer, a Classical Dictionary, a Chronology, a Law Dictionary, a Synopsis of the Peerage, useful Tables, &c. Fcp. 8vo. 10s.

General and School Atlases.

An **ELEMENTARY ATLAS of HISTORY and GEOGRAPHY**, from the commencement of the Christian Era to the Present Time, in 16 coloured Maps, chronologically arranged, with illustrative Memoirs. By the Rev. J. S. BREWER, M.A. Royal 8vo. 12s. 6d.

SCHOOL ATLAS of PHYSICAL, POLITICAL, and COMMERCIAL GEOGRAPHY, in 17 full-coloured Maps, accompanied by descriptive Letterpress. By E. HUGHES, F.R.A.S. Royal 8vo. 10s. 6d.

BISHOP BUTLER'S ATLAS of ANCIENT GEOGRAPHY, in a Series of 24 full-coloured Maps, accompanied by a complete Accentuated Index. New Edition, corrected and enlarged. Royal 8vo. 12s.

BISHOP BUTLER'S ATLAS of MODERN GEOGRAPHY, in a Series of 33 full-coloured Maps, accompanied by a complete Alphabetical Index. New Edition, corrected and enlarged. Royal 8vo. 10s. 6d.

In consequence of the rapid advance of geographical discovery, and the many recent changes, through political causes, in the boundaries of various countries, it has been found necessary thoroughly to revise this long-established Atlas, and to add several new Maps. New Maps have been given of the following countries: *Palestine, Canada,* and the adjacent provinces of *New Brunswick, Nova Scotia,* and *Newfoundland,* the *American States* bordering on the Pacific, *Eastern Australia,* and *New Zealand.* In addition to these Maps of *Western Australia* and *Tasmania* have been given in compartments; thus completing the revision of the Map of *Australasia,* rendered necessary by the rising importance of our Australasian possessions. In the Map of *Europe, Iceland* has also been re-drawn, and the new boundaries of *France, Italy,* and *Austria* represented. The Maps of the three last-named countries have been carefully revised. The Map of *Switzerland* has been wholly re-drawn, showing more accurately the physical features of the country. *Africa* has been carefully compared with the discoveries of LIVINGSTONE, BURTON, SPEKE, BARTH, and other explorers. The number of Maps is thus raised from Thirty to Thirty-three. An entirely new INDEX has been constructed; and the price of the work has been reduced from 12s. to Half-a-Guinea. The present edition, therefore, will be found much superior to former ones; and the Publishers feel assured that it will maintain the character which this work has so long enjoyed as a popular and comprehensive School Atlas.

MIDDLE-CLASS ATLAS of GENERAL GEOGRAPHY, in a Series of 29 full-coloured Maps, containing the most recent Territorial Changes and Discoveries. By WALTER M'LEOD, F.R.G.S. 4to. 5s.

PHYSICAL ATLAS of GREAT BRITAIN and IRELAND; comprising 30 full-coloured Maps, with illustrative Letterpress, forming a Concise Synopsis of British Physical Geography. By WALTER M'LEOD, F.R.G.S. Fcp. 4to. 7s. 6d.

Periodical Publications.

The EDINBURGH REVIEW, or **CRITICAL JOURNAL,** published Quarterly in January, April, July, and October. 8vo. price 6s. each No.

The GEOLOGICAL MAGAZINE, or Monthly Journal of Geology, edited by T. RUPERT JONES, F.G.S. assisted by HENRY WOODWARD, F.G.S. 8vo. price 1s. 6d. each No.

FRASER'S MAGAZINE for TOWN and COUNTRY, published on the 1st of each Month. 8vo. price 2s. 6d. each No.

The ALPINE JOURNAL: a Record of Mountain Adventure and Scientific Observation. By Members of the Alpine Club. Edited by H. R. GEORGE, M.A. Published Quarterly, May 31, Aug. 31, Nov. 30, Feb. 28. 8vo. price 1s. 6d. each No.

INDEX.

SPOTTISWOODE AND CO., PRINTERS, NEW-STREET SQUARE, LONDON

www.ingramcontent.com/pod-product-compliance
Lightning Source LLC
Chambersburg PA
CBHW030539270326
41927CB00008B/1437